Dress Your Family in Corduroy and Denim

*Also by David Sedaris
in Large Print:*

Me Talk Pretty One Day

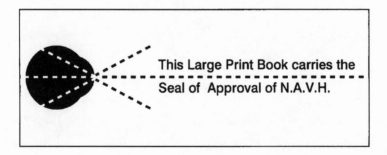

Dress Your Family in Corduroy and Denim

David Sedaris

Thorndike Press • Waterville, Maine

Acknowledgment is made to the following, in which the stories in this collection were originally published, some differently titled or in slightly different form: *Esquire*: "Repeat After Me," "Consider the Stars," "Rooster at the Hitchin' Post," "Six to Eight Black Men," "The End of the Affair," and "Full House"; *G.Q.*: "Slumus Lordicus," "The Change in Me," "Put a Lid on It," "Monie Changes Everything," and "Baby Einstein"; and *The New Yorker*: "The Girl Next Door," "The Ship Shape," "Who's the Chef?," "Us and Them," "Let It Snow," "Nuit of the Living Dead," "Possession," and "Blood Work." "A Can of Worms" and "Hejira" were originally broadcast on "This American Life."

Author's note: The events described in these stories are real. Certain characters have fictitious names and identifying characteristics.

Published in 2004 by arrangement with Little, Brown and Company, Inc.

Thorndike Press® Large Print Core.

The tree indicium is a trademark of Thorndike Press.

The text of this Large Print edition is unabridged. Other aspects of the book may vary from the original edition.

Set in 16 pt. Plantin by Elena Picard.

Printed in the United States on permanent paper.

Library of Congress Cataloging-in-Publication Data

Sedaris, David.
    Dress your family in corduroy and denim / David Sedaris.
      p. cm.
    ISBN 0-7862-6950-2 (lg. print : hc : alk. paper)
    1. Large type books.   I. Title.
PS3569.E314D74 2004
  813′.54—dc22   2004055342

For Hugh

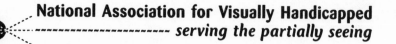

National Association for Visually Handicapped
serving the partially seeing

As the Founder/CEO of NAVH, the only national health agency solely devoted to those who, although not totally blind, have an eye disease which could lead to serious visual impairment, I am pleased to recognize Thorndike Press★ as one of the leading publishers in the large print field.

Founded in 1954 in San Francisco to prepare large print textbooks for partially seeing children, NAVH became the pioneer and standard setting agency in the preparation of large type.

Today, those publishers who meet our standards carry the prestigious "Seal of Approval" indicating high quality large print. We are delighted that Thorndike Press is one of the publishers whose titles meet these standards. We are also pleased to recognize the significant contribution Thorndike Press is making in this important and growing field.

Lorraine H. Marchi, L.H.D.
Founder/CEO
NAVH

★ Thorndike Press encompasses the following imprints: Thorndike, Wheeler, Walker and Large Print Press.

Contents

Grateful acknowledgment is offered to the various editors I consider myself lucky to have worked with: Jeffrey Frank at *The New Yorker*, Ira Glass at "This American Life," Maja Thomas and Steve Lamont at Little, Brown, and Andy Ward at *Esquire* and *G.Q.*

Us and Them

When my family first moved to North Carolina, we lived in a rented house three blocks from the school where I would begin the third grade. My mother made friends with one of the neighbors, but one seemed enough for her. Within a year we would move again and, as she explained, there wasn't much point in getting too close to people we would have to say good-bye to. Our next house was less than a mile away, and the short journey would hardly merit tears or even good-byes, for that matter. It was more of a "see you later" situation, but still I adopted my mother's attitude, as it allowed me to pretend that not making friends was a conscious choice. I could if I wanted to. It just wasn't the right time.

Back in New York State, we had lived in the country, with no sidewalks or streetlights; you could leave the house and still be alone. But here, when you looked out the window, you saw other houses, and people inside those houses. I hoped that in

9

walking around after dark I might witness a murder, but for the most part our neighbors just sat in their living rooms, watching TV. The only place that seemed truly different was owned by a man named Mr. Tomkey, who did not believe in television. This was told to us by our mother's friend, who dropped by one afternoon with a basketful of okra. The woman did not editorialize — rather, she just presented her information, leaving her listener to make of it what she might. Had my mother said, "That's the craziest thing I've ever heard in my life," I assume that the friend would have agreed, and had she said, "Three cheers for Mr. Tomkey," the friend likely would have agreed as well. It was a kind of test, as was the okra.

To say that you did not believe in television was different from saying that you did not care for it. Belief implied that television had a master plan and that you were against it. It also suggested that you thought too much. When my mother reported that Mr. Tomkey did not believe in television, my father said, "Well, good for him. I don't know that I believe in it, either."

"That's exactly how I feel," my mother said, and then my parents watched the

10

news, and whatever came on after the news.

Word spread that Mr. Tomkey did not own a television, and you began hearing that while this was all very well and good, it was unfair of him to inflict his beliefs upon others, specifically his innocent wife and children. It was speculated that just as the blind man develops a keener sense of hearing, the family must somehow compensate for their loss. "Maybe they read," my mother's friend said. "Maybe they listen to the radio, but you can bet your boots they're doing *something*."

I wanted to know what this something was, and so I began peering through the Tomkeys' windows. During the day I'd stand across the street from their house, acting as though I were waiting for someone, and at night, when the view was better and I had less chance of being discovered, I would creep into their yard and hide in the bushes beside their fence.

Because they had no TV, the Tomkeys were forced to talk during dinner. They had no idea how puny their lives were, and so they were not ashamed that a camera would have found them uninteresting. They did not know what attractive was or

11

what dinner was supposed to look like or even what time people were supposed to eat. Sometimes they wouldn't sit down until eight o'clock, long after everyone else had finished doing the dishes. During the meal, Mr. Tomkey would occasionally pound the table and point at his children with a fork, but the moment he finished, everyone would start laughing. I got the idea that he was imitating someone else, and wondered if he spied on us while we were eating.

When fall arrived and school began, I saw the Tomkey children marching up the hill with paper sacks in their hands. The son was one grade lower than me, and the daughter was one grade higher. We never spoke, but I'd pass them in the halls from time to time and attempt to view the world through their eyes. What must it be like to be so ignorant and alone? Could a normal person even imagine it? Staring at an Elmer Fudd lunch box, I tried to divorce myself from everything I already knew: Elmer's inability to pronounce the letter *r*, his constant pursuit of an intelligent and considerably more famous rabbit. I tried to think of him as just a drawing, but it was impossible to separate him from his celebrity.

One day in class a boy named William began to write the wrong answer on the blackboard, and our teacher flailed her arms, saying, "Warning, Will. Danger, danger." Her voice was synthetic and void of emotion, and we laughed, knowing that she was imitating the robot in a weekly show about a family who lived in outer space. The Tomkeys, though, would have thought she was having a heart attack. It occurred to me that they needed a guide, someone who could accompany them through the course of an average day and point out all the things they were unable to understand. I could have done it on weekends, but friendship would have taken away their mystery and interfered with the good feeling I got from pitying them. So I kept my distance.

In early October the Tomkeys bought a boat, and everyone seemed greatly relieved, especially my mother's friend, who noted that the motor was definitely secondhand. It was reported that Mr. Tomkey's father-in-law owned a house on the lake and had invited the family to use it whenever they liked. This explained why they were gone all weekend, but it did not make their absences any easier to bear. I felt as if my favorite show had been canceled.

Halloween fell on a Saturday that year, and by the time my mother took us to the store, all the good costumes were gone. My sisters dressed as witches and I went as a hobo. I'd looked forward to going in disguise to the Tomkeys' door, but they were off at the lake, and their house was dark. Before leaving, they had left a coffee can full of gumdrops on the front porch, alongside a sign reading DON'T BE GREEDY. In terms of Halloween candy, individual gumdrops were just about as low as you could get. This was evidenced by the large number of them floating in an adjacent dog bowl. It was disgusting to think that this was what a gumdrop might look like in your stomach, and it was insulting to be told not to take too much of something you didn't really want in the first place. "Who do these Tomkeys think they are?" my sister Lisa said.

The night after Halloween, we were sitting around watching TV when the doorbell rang. Visitors were infrequent at our house, so while my father stayed behind, my mother, sisters, and I ran downstairs in a group, opening the door to discover the entire Tomkey family on our front stoop.

The parents looked as they always had, but the son and daughter were dressed in costumes — she as a ballerina and he as some kind of a rodent with terry-cloth ears and a tail made from what looked to be an extension cord. It seemed they had spent the previous evening isolated at the lake and had missed the opportunity to observe Halloween. "So, well, I guess we're trick-or-treating *now*, if that's okay," Mr. Tomkey said.

I attributed their behavior to the fact that they didn't have a TV, but television didn't teach you everything. Asking for candy on Halloween was called trick-or-treating, but asking for candy on November first was called begging, and it made people uncomfortable. This was one of the things you were supposed to learn simply by being alive, and it angered me that the Tomkeys did not understand it.

"Why of course it's not too late," my mother said. "Kids, why don't you . . . run and get . . . the candy."

"But the candy is gone," my sister Gretchen said. "You gave it away last night."

"Not *that* candy," my mother said. "The other candy. Why don't you run and go get it?"

"You mean *our* candy?" Lisa said. "The candy that we *earned?*"

This was exactly what our mother was talking about, but she didn't want to say this in front of the Tomkeys. In order to spare their feelings, she wanted them to believe that we always kept a bucket of candy lying around the house, just waiting for someone to knock on the door and ask for it. "Go on, now," she said. "Hurry up."

My room was situated right off the foyer, and if the Tomkeys had looked in that direction, they could have seen my bed and the brown paper bag marked MY CANDY. KEEP OUT. I didn't want them to know how much I had, and so I went into my room and shut the door behind me. Then I closed the curtains and emptied my bag onto the bed, searching for whatever was the crummiest. All my life chocolate has made me ill. I don't know if I'm allergic or what, but even the smallest amount leaves me with a blinding headache. Eventually, I learned to stay away from it, but as a child I refused to be left out. The brownies were eaten, and when the pounding began I would blame the grape juice or my mother's cigarette smoke or the tightness of my glasses — anything but the chocolate. My candy bars were poison but they were brand-name, and so I put them in pile no. 1, which definitely would not go to the Tomkeys.

Out in the hallway I could hear my mother straining for something to talk about. "A boat!" she said. "That sounds marvelous. Can you just drive it right into the water?"

"Actually, we have a trailer," Mr. Tomkey said. "So what we do is back it into the lake."

"Oh, a trailer. What kind is it?"

"Well, it's a *boat* trailer," Mr. Tomkey said.

"Right, but is it wooden or, you know . . . I guess what I'm asking is what *style* trailer do you have?"

Behind my mother's words were two messages. The first and most obvious was "Yes, I am talking about boat trailers, but also I am dying." The second, meant only for my sisters and me, was "If you do not immediately step forward with that candy, you will never again experience freedom, happiness, or the possibility of my warm embrace."

I knew that it was just a matter of time before she came into my room and started collecting the candy herself, grabbing indiscriminately, with no regard to my rating

17

system. Had I been thinking straight, I would have hidden the most valuable items in my dresser drawer, but instead, panicked by the thought of her hand on my doorknob, I tore off the wrappers and began cramming the candy bars into my mouth, desperately, like someone in a contest. Most were miniature, which made them easier to accommodate, but still there was only so much room, and it was hard to chew and fit more in at the same time. The headache began immediately, and I chalked it up to tension.

My mother told the Tomkeys she needed to check on something, and then she opened the door and stuck her head inside my room. "What the *hell* are you doing?" she whispered, but my mouth was too full to answer. "I'll just be a moment," she called, and as she closed the door behind her and moved toward my bed, I began breaking the wax lips and candy necklaces pulled from pile no. 2. These were the second-best things I had received, and while it hurt to destroy them, it would have hurt even more to give them away. I had just started to mutilate a miniature box of Red Hots when my mother pried them from my hands, accidentally finishing the job for me. BB-size pellets clattered onto the floor, and as I followed them with my eyes, she snatched up a roll of Necco wafers.

"Not those," I pleaded, but rather than words, my mouth expelled chocolate, chewed chocolate, which fell onto the sleeve of her sweater. "Not those. Not those."

She shook her arm, and the mound of chocolate dropped like a horrible turd upon my bedspread. "You should look at yourself," she said. "I mean, *really* look at yourself."

Along with the Necco wafers she took several Tootsie Pops and half a dozen caramels wrapped in cellophane. I heard her apologize to the Tomkeys for her absence, and then I heard my candy hitting the bottom of their bags.

"What do you say?" Mrs. Tomkey asked.

And the children answered, "Thank you."

While I was in trouble for not bringing my candy sooner, my sisters were in more trouble for not bringing theirs at all. We spent the early part of the evening in our rooms, then one by one we eased our way back upstairs, and joined our parents in front of the TV. I was the last to arrive, and took a seat on the floor beside the sofa. The show was a Western, and even if my head had not been throbbing, I doubt I would have had the wherewithal to follow it. A posse of outlaws crested a rocky hilltop, squinting at a flurry of dust advancing from the horizon, and I thought again of the Tomkeys and of how alone and out of place they had looked in their dopey costumes. "What was up with that kid's tail?" I asked.

"Shhhh," my family said.

For months I had protected and watched over these people, but now, with one stupid act, they had turned my pity into something hard and ugly. The shift wasn't gradual, but immediate, and it provoked an uncomfortable feeling of loss. We hadn't been friends, the Tomkeys and I, but still I had given them the gift of my curiosity. Wondering about the Tomkey family had made me feel generous, but now I would have to shift gears and find pleasure in hating them. The only alternative was to do as my mother had instructed and take a good look at myself. This was an old trick, designed to turn one's hatred inward, and while I was determined not to fall for it, it was hard to shake the mental picture snapped by her suggestion: here is a boy sitting on a bed, his mouth smeared with chocolate. He's a human being, but also he's a pig, surrounded by trash and gorging himself so that others may be denied. Were this the only image in the world, you'd be forced to give it your full attention, but fortunately there were others. This stagecoach, for instance, coming round the bend with a cargo of gold. This shiny new Mustang convertible. This teenage girl, her hair a beautiful mane, sipping Pepsi through a straw, one picture after another, on and on until the news, and whatever came on after the news.

Let It Snow

In Binghamton, New York, winter meant snow, and though I was young when we left, I was able to recall great heaps of it, and use that memory as evidence that North Carolina was, at best, a third-rate institution. What little snow there was would usually melt an hour or two after hitting the ground, and there you'd be in your windbreaker and unconvincing mittens, forming a lumpy figure made mostly of mud. Snow Negroes, we called them.

The winter I was in the fifth grade we got lucky. Snow fell, and for the first time in years, it accumulated. School was canceled and two days later we got lucky again. There were eight inches on the ground, and rather than melting, it froze. On the fifth day of our vacation my mother had a little breakdown. Our presence had disrupted the secret life she led while we were at school, and when she could no longer take it she threw us out. It wasn't a gentle request, but something closer to an eviction. "Get the hell out of my house," she said.

We reminded her that it was our house, too, and she opened the front door and shoved us into the carport. "And stay out!" she shouted.

My sisters and I went down the hill and sledded with other children from the neighborhood. A few hours later we returned home, surprised to find that the door was still locked. "Oh, come on," we said. I rang the bell and when no one answered we went to the window and saw our mother in the kitchen, watching television. Normally she waited until five o'clock to have a drink, but for the past few days she'd been making an exception. Drinking didn't count if you followed a glass of wine with a cup of coffee, and so she had both a goblet and a mug positioned before her on the countertop.

"Hey!" we yelled. "Open the door. It's us." We knocked on the pane, and without looking in our direction, she refilled her goblet and left the room.

"That bitch," my sister Lisa said. We pounded again and again, and when our mother failed to answer we went around back and threw snowballs at her bedroom window. "You are going to be in so much trouble when Dad gets home!" we shouted, and in response my mother pulled the drapes. Dusk approached, and as it grew colder it occurred to us that we could possibly die. It happened, surely. Selfish mothers wanted the house to themselves, and their children were discovered years later, frozen like mastodons in blocks of ice.

My sister Gretchen suggested that we call our father, but none of us knew his number, and he probably wouldn't have done anything anyway. He'd gone to work specifically to escape our mother, and between the weather and her mood, it could be hours or even days before he returned home.

"One of us should get hit by a car," I said. "That would teach the both of them." I pictured Gretchen, her life hanging by a thread as my parents paced the halls of Rex Hospital, wishing they had been more attentive. It was really the perfect solution. With her out of the way, the rest of us would be more valuable and have a bit more room to spread out. "Gretchen, go lie in the street."

"Make Amy do it," she said.

Amy, in turn, pushed it off onto Tiffany, who was the youngest and had no concept of death. "It's like sleeping," we told her. "Only you get a canopy bed."

Poor Tiffany. She'd do just about anything in return for a little affection. All you had to do was call her Tiff and whatever you wanted was yours: her allowance money, her dinner, the contents of her Easter basket. Her eagerness to please was absolute and naked. When we asked her to lie in the middle of the street, her only question was "Where?"

We chose a quiet dip between two hills, a spot where drivers were almost required to skid out of control. She took her place, this six-year-old in a butter-colored coat, and we gathered on the curb to watch. The first car to happen by belonged to a neighbor, a fellow Yankee who had outfitted his tires with chains and stopped a few feet from our sister's body. "Is that a person?" he asked.

"Well, sort of," Lisa said. She explained that we'd been locked out of our house and though the man appeared to accept it as a reasonable explanation, I'm pretty sure it was him who told on us. Another car passed and then we saw our mother, this puffy figure awkwardly negotiating the crest of the hill. She did not own a pair of pants, and her legs were buried to the calves in snow. We wanted to send her home, to kick her out of nature just as she had kicked us out of the house, but it was hard to stay angry at someone that pitiful-looking.

"Are you wearing your *loafers?*" Lisa asked, and in response our mother raised her bare foot. "I *was* wearing loafers," she said. "I mean, really, it was there a second ago."

This was how things went. One moment she was locking us out of our own house and the next we were rooting around in the snow, looking for her left shoe. "Oh, forget about it," she said. "It'll turn up in a few days." Gretchen fitted her cap over my mother's foot. Lisa secured it with her scarf, and surrounding her tightly on all sides, we made our way back home.

The Ship Shape

My mother and I were at the dry cleaner's, standing behind a woman we had never seen. "A nice-looking woman," my mother would later say. "Well put together. Classy." The woman was dressed for the season in a light cotton shift patterned with oversize daisies. Her shoes matched the petals and her purse, which was black-and-yellow-striped, hung over her shoulder, buzzing the flowers like a lazy bumblebee. She handed in her claim check, accepted her garments, and then expressed gratitude for what she considered to be fast and efficient service. "You know," she said, "people talk about Raleigh, but it isn't really true, is it?"

The Korean man nodded, the way you do when you're a foreigner and understand that someone has finished a sentence. He wasn't the owner, just a helper who'd stepped in from the back, and it was clear he had no idea what she was saying.

"My sister and I are visiting from out of town," the woman said, a little louder now, and again the man nodded. "I'd love to stay awhile longer and explore, but my home — well, *one* of my homes — is on the garden tour, so I've got to get back to Williamsburg."

I was eleven years old, yet still the statement seemed strange to me. If she'd hoped to impress the Korean, the woman had obviously wasted her breath, so who was this information for?

"My home — well, *one* of my homes": by the end of the day my mother and I had repeated this line no less than fifty times. The garden tour was unimportant, but the first part of her sentence brought us great pleasure. There was, as indicated by the dash, a pause between the words *home* and *well*, a brief moment in which she'd decided, *Oh, why not?* The following word — *one* — had blown from her mouth as if propelled by a gentle breeze, and this was the difficult part. You had to get it just right, or else the sentence lost its power. Falling somewhere between a self-conscious laugh and a sigh of happy confusion, the *one* afforded her statement a double meaning. To her peers it meant "Look at me, I catch myself coming and going!" and to the less fortunate it was a way of saying, "Don't kid yourself, it's a lot of work having more than one house."

The first dozen times we tried it, our voices sounded pinched and snobbish, but by midafternoon they had softened. We wanted what this woman had. Mocking her made it seem hopelessly unobtainable, and so we reverted to our natural selves.

"My home — well, one of my homes . . ." My mother said it in a rush, as if she were under pressure to be more specific. It was the same way she said, "My daughter — well, one of my daughters," but a second home was more prestigious than a second daughter, and so it didn't really work. I went in the opposite direction, exaggerating the word *one* in a way that was guaranteed to alienate my listener.

"Say it like that and people are going to be jealous," my mother said.

"Well, isn't that what we want?"

"Sort of," she said. "But mainly we want them to be happy for us."

"But why should you be happy for someone who has more than you do?"

"I guess it all depends on the person," she said. "Anyway, I suppose it doesn't matter. We'll get it right eventually. When the day arrives, I'm sure it'll just come to us."

And so we waited.

★ ★ ★

At some point in the mid to late 1960s, North Carolina began referring to itself as "Variety Vacationland." The words were stamped onto license plates, and a series of television commercials reminded us that, unlike certain of our neighbors, we had both the beach *and* the mountains. There were those who bounced back and forth between one and the other, but most people tended to choose a landscape and stick to it. We ourselves were Beach People, Emerald Isle People, but that was mainly my mother's doing. I don't think our father would have cared whether he took a vacation or not. Being away from home left him anxious and crabby, but our mother loved the ocean. She couldn't swim, but enjoyed standing at the water's edge with a pole in her hand. It wasn't exactly what you'd call fishing, as she caught nothing and expressed neither hope nor disappointment in regard to her efforts. What she thought about while looking at the waves was a complete mystery, yet you could tell that these thoughts pleased her, and that she liked herself better while thinking them.

One year our father waited too late to make our reservations, and we were forced to take something on the sound. It wasn't a cottage but a run-down house, the sort of place where poor people lived. The yard was enclosed by a chain-link fence, and the air was thick with the flies and mosquitoes normally blown away by the ocean breezes. Midway through the vacation a hideous woolly caterpillar fell from a tree and bit my sister Amy on the cheek. Her face swelled and discolored, and within an hour, were it not for her arms and legs, it would have been difficult to recognize her as a human. My mother drove her to the hospital, and when they returned she employed my sister as Exhibit A, pointing as if this were not her daughter but some ugly stranger forced to share our quarters. "*This* is what you get for waiting until the last minute," she said to our father. "No dunes, no waves, just *this*."

From that year on, our mother handled the reservations. We went to Emerald Isle for a week every September and were always oceanfront, a word that suggested a certain degree of entitlement. The oceanfront cottages were on stilts, which made them appear if not large, then at least imposing. Some were painted, some were sided "Cape Cod style" with wooden shingles, and all of them had names, the cleverest being Loafer's Paradise. The owners had cut their sign in the shape of two moccasins resting side by side. The shoes were realistically painted and the letters were bloated and listless, loitering like drunks against the soft faux leather.

"Now *that's* a sign," our father would say, and we would agree. There was The Skinny Dipper, Pelican's Perch, Lazy Daze, The Scotch Bonnet, Loony Dunes, the name of each house followed by the name and hometown of the owner. "The Duncan Clan — Charlotte," "The Graftons — Rocky Mount," "Hal and Jean Starling of Pinehurst" — signs that essentially said, "My home — well, *one* of my homes."

While at the beach we sensed more than ever that our lives were governed by luck. When we had it — when it was sunny — my sisters and I felt as if we were somehow personally responsible. We were a fortunate family, and therefore everyone around us was allowed to swim and dig in the sand. When it rained, we were unlucky, and stayed indoors to search our souls. "It'll clear after lunch," our mother would say, and we would eat carefully, using the place mats that had brought us luck in the past. When that failed, we would move on to Plan B. "Oh, Mother, you work too hard," we'd say. "Let *us* do the dishes. Let *us* sweep sand off the floor." We spoke like children in a fairy tale, hoping our goodness might lure the sun from its hiding place. "You and Father have been so kind to us. Here, let us massage your shoulders."

If by late afternoon it still hadn't cleared, my sisters and I would drop the act and turn on one another, searching for the spoiler who had brought us this misfortune. Which of us seemed the least dissatisfied? Who had curled up on a mildewed bed with a book and a glass of chocolate milk, behaving as though the rain were not such a bad thing after all? We would find this person, most often my sister Gretchen, and then we would beat her.

The summer I was twelve a tropical storm moved up the coast, leaving a sky the same mottled pewter as Gretchen's subsequent bruises, but the following year we started with luck. My father found a golf course that suited him, and for the first time in memory even he seemed to enjoy himself. Relaxing on the deck with a gin and tonic, surrounded by his toast-colored wife and children, he admitted that this really wasn't so bad. "I've been thinking, to hell with these rental cottages," he said. "What do you say we skip the middleman and just buy a place."

He spoke in the same tone he used when promising ice cream. "Who's up for something sweet?" he'd ask, and we'd pile into the car, passing the Tastee Freeze and driving to the grocery store, where he'd buy a block of pus-colored ice milk reduced for quick sale. Experience had taught us not to trust him, but we wanted a beach house so badly it was impossible not to get caught up in the excitement. Even our mother fell for it.

"Do you really mean this?" she asked.

"Absolutely," he said.

The next day they made an appointment with a real-estate agent in Morehead City. "We'll just be discussing the possibility," my mother said. "It's just a meeting, nothing more." We wanted to join them but they took only Paul, who was two years old and unfit to be left in our company. The morning meeting led to half a dozen viewings, and when they returned, my mother's face was so impassive it seemed almost paralyzed. "It-was-fine," she said. "The-real-estate-agent-was-very-nice." We got the idea that she was under oath to keep something to herself and that the effort was causing her actual physical pain.

"It's all right," my father said. "You can tell them."

"Well, we saw this one place in particular," she told us. "Now, it's nothing to get worked up about, but . . ."

"But it's perfect," my father said. "A real beauty, just like your mother here." He came from behind and pinched her on the bottom. She laughed and swatted him with a towel, and we witnessed what we would later come to recognize as the rejuvenating power of real estate. It's what fortunate couples turn to when their sex life has faded and they're too pious for affairs. A second car might bring people together for a week or two, but a second home can revitalize a marriage for up to nine months after the closing.

"Oh, Lou," my mother said. "What am I going to do with you?"

"Whatever you want, baby," he said. "Whatever you want."

It was queer when people repeated their sentences twice, but we were willing to overlook it in exchange for a beach house. My mother was too excited to cook that night, and so we ate dinner at the Sanitary Fish Market in Morehead City. On taking our seats I expected my father to mention inadequate insulation or corroded pipes, the dark undersides of home ownership, but instead he discussed only the positive aspects. "I don't see why we couldn't spend our Thanksgivings here. Hell, we could even come for Christmas. Hang a few lights, get some ornaments, what do you think?"

A waitress passed the table, and without saying please, I demanded another Coke. She went to fetch it, and I settled back in my chair, drunk with the power of a second home. When school began, my classmates would court me, hoping I might invite them for a weekend, and I would make a game of pitting them against one another. This was what a person did when people liked him for all the wrong reasons, and I would grow to be very good at it.

"What do you think, David?" my father asked. I hadn't heard the question but said that it sounded good to me. "I like it," I said. "I like it."

The following afternoon our parents took us to see the house. "Now, I don't want you to get your hopes up too high," my mother said, but it was too late for that. It was a fifteen-minute drive from one end of the island to the other, and along the way we proposed names for what we had come to think of as our cottage. I'd already given it a good deal of thought but waited a few minutes before offering my suggestion.

"Are you ready?" I said. "Our sign will be the silhouette of a ship."

Nobody said anything.

"Get it?" I said. "The shape of a ship. Our house will be called The Ship Shape."

"Well, you'd have to write that on the sign," my father said. "Otherwise, nobody will get it."

"But if you write out the words you'll ruin the joke."

"What about The Nut Hut?" Amy said.

"Hey!" my father said. "Now there's an idea." He laughed, not realizing, I guess, that there already was a Nut Hut. We'd passed it a thousand times.

"How about something with the word *sandpiper* in it," my mother said. "Everybody likes sandpipers, right?"

Normally I would have hated them for not recognizing my suggestion as the best, but this was clearly a special time and I didn't want to ruin it with brooding. Each of us wanted to be the one who came up with the name, and inspiration could be hiding anywhere. When the interior of the car had been exhausted of ideas, we looked out the windows and searched the passing landscape.

Two thin girls braced themselves before crossing the busy road, hopping from foot to foot on the scalding pavement. "The Tar Heel," Lisa called out. "No, The Wait 'n' Sea. Get it? S-E-A."

A car trailing a motorboat pulled up to a gas pump. "The Shell Station!" Gretchen shouted.

Everything we saw was offered as a possible name, and the resulting list of nominees confirmed that once you left the shoreline, Emerald Isle was sorely lacking in natural beauty. "The TV Antenna," my sister Tiffany said. "The Telephone Pole." "The Toothless Black Man Selling Shrimp from the Back of His Van."

"The Cement Mixer." "The Overturned Grocery Cart." "Gulls on a Garbage Can." My mother inspired "The Cigarette Butt Thrown Out the Window" and suggested we look for ideas on the beach rather than on the highway. "I mean, my God, how depressing can you get?" She acted annoyed, but we could tell she was really enjoying it. "Give me something that suits us," she said. "Give me something that will last."

What would ultimately last were these fifteen minutes on the coastal highway, but we didn't know that then. When older, even the crankiest of us would accept them as proof that we were once a happy family: our mother young and healthy, our father the man who could snap his fingers and give us everything we wanted, the whole lot of us competing to name our good fortune.

The house was, as our parents had promised, perfect. This was an older cottage with pine-paneled walls that gave each room the thoughtful quality of a den. Light fell in strips from the louvered shutters, and the furniture, which was included in the sale, reflected the taste of a distinguished sea captain. Once we'd claimed bedrooms and lain awake all night, mentally rearranging the furniture, it would be our father who'd say, "Now hold on a minute, it's not ours *yet.*" By the next afternoon he had decided that the golf course wasn't so great after all. Then it rained for two straight days, and he announced that it might be wiser to buy some land, wait a few years, and think about building a place of our own. "I mean, let's be practical." Our mother put on her raincoat. She tied a plastic bag over her head and stood at the water's edge, and for the first time in our lives we knew exactly what she was thinking.

By our final day of vacation our father had decided that instead of building a place on Emerald Isle, we should improve the home we already had. "Maybe add a pool," he said. "What do you kids think about that?" Nobody answered.

By the time he'd finished wheedling it down, the house at the beach had become a bar in the basement. It looked just like a real bar, with tall stools and nooks for wine. There was a sink for washing glasses and an assortment of cartoon napkins illustrating the lighter side of alcoholism. For a week or two my sisters and I tottered at the counter, pretending to be drunks, but then the novelty wore off and we forgot all about it.

On subsequent vacations, both with and without our parents, we would drive by the cottage we had once thought of as our own. Each of us referred to it by a different name, and over time qualifiers became necessary. ("You know, *our* house.") The summer after we didn't buy it, the new owners — or "those people," as we liked to call them — painted The Ship Shape yellow. In the late seventies Amy noted that

The Nut Hut had extended the carport and paved the driveway. Lisa was relieved when the Wait 'n' Sea returned to its original color, and Tiffany was incensed when The Toothless Black Man Selling Shrimp from the Back of His Van sported a sign endorsing Jesse Helms in the 1984 senatorial campaign. Four years later my mother called to report that The Sandpiper had been badly damaged by Hurricane Hugo. "It's still there," she said. "But barely." Shortly thereafter, according to Gretchen, The Shell Station was torn down and sold as a vacant lot.

I know that such a story does not quite work to inspire sympathy. ("My home — well, *one* of my homes — fell through.") We had no legitimate claim to self-pity, were ineligible even to hold a grudge, but that didn't stop us from complaining.

In the coming years our father would continue to promise what he couldn't deliver, and in time we grew to think of him as an actor auditioning for the role of a benevolent millionaire. He'd never get the part but liked the way that the words felt in his mouth. "What do you say to a new car?" he'd ask. "Who's up for a cruise to the Greek Isles?" He expected us to respond by playing the part of an enthusiastic family, but we were unwilling to resume our old roles. As if carried by a tide, our mother drifted farther and farther away, first to twin beds and then down the hall to a room decorated with seascapes and baskets of sun-bleached sand dollars. It would have been nice, a place at the beach, but we already had a home. A home with a bar. Besides, had things worked out, you wouldn't have been happy for us. We're not that kind of people.

Full House

My parents were not the type of people who went to bed at a regular hour. Sleep overtook them, but neither the time nor the idea of a mattress seemed very important. My father favored a chair in the basement, but my mother was apt to lie down anywhere, waking with carpet burns on her face or the pattern of the sofa embossed into the soft flesh of her upper arms. It was sort of embarrassing. She might sleep for eight hours a day, but they were never consecutive hours and they involved no separate outfit. For Christmas we would give her nightgowns, hoping she might take the hint. "They're for bedtime," we'd say, and she'd look at us strangely, as if, like the moment of one's death, the occasion of sleep was too incalculable to involve any real preparation.

The upside to being raised by what were essentially a pair of house cats was that we never had any enforced bedtime. At two a.m. on a school night, my mother would not say, "Go to sleep," but rather,

"Shouldn't you be tired?" It wasn't a command but a sincere question, the answer provoking little more than a shrug. "Suit yourself," she'd say, pouring what was likely to be her thirtieth or forty-second cup of coffee. "I'm not sleepy, either. Don't know why, but I'm not."

We were the family that never shut down, the family whose TV was so hot we needed an oven mitt in order to change the channel. Every night was basically a slumber party, so when the real thing came along, my sisters and I failed to show much of an interest.

"But we get to stay up as late as we want," the hosts would say.

"And . . . ?"

The first one I attended was held by a neighbor named Walt Winters. Like me, Walt was in the sixth grade. Unlike me, he was gregarious and athletic, which meant, basically, that we had absolutely nothing in common. "But why would he include *me?*" I asked my mother. "I hardly know the guy."

She did not say that Walt's mother had made him invite me, but I knew that this was the only likely explanation. "Oh, go," she said. "It'll be fun."

I tried my best to back out, but then my

father got wind of it, and that option was closed. He often passed Walt playing football in the street and saw in the boy a younger version of himself. "He's maybe not the best player in the world, but he and his friends, they're a good group."

"Fine," I said. "Then *you* go sleep with them."

I could not tell my father that boys made me anxious, and so I invented individual reasons to dislike them. The hope was that I might seem discerning rather than frightened, but instead I came off sounding like a prude.

"You're expecting me to spend the night with someone who curses? Someone who actually throws *rocks* at *cats?*"

"You're damned right I am," my father said. "Now get the hell over there."

Aside from myself, there were three other guests at Walt's slumber party. None of them were particularly popular — they weren't good-looking enough for that — but each could hold his own on a playing field or in a discussion about cars. The talk started the moment I walked through the door, and while pretending to listen, I wished that I could have been more honest. "What is the actual point of football?" I wanted to ask. "Is a V-8 engine related in any way to the juice?" I would have sounded like a foreign-exchange student, but the answers might have given me some sort of a foundation. As it was, they may as well have been talking backward.

There were four styles of houses on our street, and while Walt's was different from my own, I was familiar with the layout. The slumber party took place in what the Methodists called a family room, the Catholics used as an extra bedroom, and the neighborhood's only Jews had turned into a combination darkroom and fallout shelter. Walt's family was Methodist, and so the room's focal point was a large black-and-white television. Family photos hung on the wall alongside pictures of the various athletes Mr. Winters had successfully pestered for autographs. I admired them to the best of my ability but was more interested in the wedding portrait displayed above the sofa. Arm in arm with her uniformed husband, Walt's mother looked deliriously, almost frighteningly happy. The bulging eyes and fierce, gummy smile: it was an expression bordering on hysteria, and the intervening years had done nothing to dampen it.

"What is she *on?*" my mother would

whisper whenever we passed Mrs. Winters waving gaily from her front yard. I thought she was being too hard on her, but after ten minutes in the woman's home I understood exactly what my mother was talking about.

"Pizza's here!!!" she chimed when the deliveryman came to the door. "Oh, boys, how about some piping hot pizza!!!" I thought it was funny that anyone would use the words *piping hot,* but it wasn't the kind of thing I felt I could actually laugh at. Neither could I laugh at Mr. Winters's pathetic imitation of an Italian waiter. "Mamma mia. Who want anudda slice a dipizza!"

I had the idea that adults were supposed to make themselves scarce at slumber parties, but Walt's parents were all over the place: initiating games, offering snacks and refills. When the midnight horror movie came on, Walt's mother crept into the bathroom, leaving a ketchup-spattered knife beside the sink. An hour passed, and when none of us had yet discovered it, she started dropping little hints. "Doesn't anyone want to wash their hands?" she asked. "Will whoever's closest to the door go check to see if I left fresh towels in the bathroom?"

You just wanted to cry for people like her.

As corny as they were, I was sorry when the movie ended and Mr. and Mrs. Winters stood to leave. It was only two a.m., but clearly they were done in. "I just don't know how you boys can do it," Walt's mother said, yawning into the sleeve of her bathrobe. "I haven't been up this late since Lauren came into the world." Lauren was Walt's sister, who was born prematurely and lived for less than two days. This had happened before the Winterses moved onto our street, but it wasn't any kind of secret, and you weren't supposed to flinch upon hearing the girl's name. The baby had died too soon to pose for photographs, but still she was regarded as a full-fledged member of the family. She had a Christmas stocking the size of a mitten, and they even threw her an annual birthday party, a fact that my mother found especially creepy. "Let's hope they don't invite us," she said. "I mean, Jesus, how do you shop for a dead baby?"

I guessed it was the fear of another premature birth that kept Mrs. Winters from trying again, which was sad, as you got the sense she really wanted a lively household. You got the sense that she had an *idea* of a lively household and that the slumber party and the ketchup-covered knife were all a part of that idea. While in her presence, we had played along, but once she said good night, I understood that all bets were off.

She and her husband lumbered up the stairs, and when Walt felt certain that they were asleep, he pounced on Dale Gummerson, shouting, "Titty twister!!!" Brad Clancy joined in, and when they had finished, Dale raised his shirt, revealing nipples as crimped and ruddy as the pepperoni slices littering the forsaken pizza box.

"Oh my God," I said, realizing too late that this made me sound like a girl. The appropriate response was to laugh at Dale's misfortune, not to flutter your hands in front of your face, screeching, "What have they done to your poor nipples! Shouldn't we put some ice on them?"

Walt picked up on this immediately. "Did you just say you wanted to put ice on Dale's nipples?"

"Well, not me . . . personally," I said. "I meant, you know, generally. As a group. Or Dale could do it himself if he felt like it."

Walt's eyes wandered from my face to my chest, and then the entire slumber party was upon me. Dale had not yet regained the full use of his arms, and so he sat on my legs while Brad and Scott Marlboro pinned me to the carpet. My shirt was raised, a hand was clamped over my mouth, and Walt latched onto my nipples, twisting them back and forth as if they were a set of particularly stubborn toggle bolts. "*Now* who needs ice!" he said. "*Now* who thinks he's the goddam school nurse." I'd once felt sorry for Walt, but now, my eyes watering in pain, I understood that little Lauren was smart to have cut out early.

When finally I was freed, I went upstairs and stood at the kitchen window, my arms folded lightly against my chest. My family's house was located in a ravine. You couldn't see it from the street, but still I could make out the glow of lights spilling from the top of our driveway. It was tempting, but were I to leave now, I'd never hear the end of it. *The baby cried. The baby had to go home.* Life at school would be unbearable, so I left the window and returned to the basement, where Walt was shuffling cards against the coffee table. "Just in time," he said. "Have a seat."

I lowered myself to the floor and reached for a magazine, trying my best to act casual. "I'm not really much for games, so if it's okay with you, I think I'll just watch."

"Watch, hell," Walt said. "This is strip poker. What kind of a homo wants to sit around and watch four guys get naked?"

The logic of this was lost on me. "Well, won't we *all* sort of be watching?"

"Looking maybe, but not *watching*," Walt said. "There's a big difference."

I asked what the difference was, but nobody answered. Then Walt made a twisting motion with his fingers, and I took my place at the table, praying for a gas leak or an electrical fire — anything to save me from the catastrophe of strip poker. To the rest of the group, a naked boy was like a lamp or a bath mat, something so familiar and uninteresting that it faded into the background, but for me it was different. A naked boy was what I desired more than anything on earth, and when you were both watching and desiring, things came up, one thing in particular that was bound to stand out and ruin your life forever. "I hate to tell you," I said, "but it's against my religion to play poker."

"Yeah, right," Walt said. "What are you, Baptist?"

"Greek Orthodox."

"Well, that's a load of crap because the

Greeks invented cards," Walt said.

"Actually, I think it was the Egyptians." This from Scott, who was quickly identifying himself as the smart one.

"Greeks, Egyptians, they're all the same thing," Walt said. "Anyway, what your pooh-bah doesn't know won't hurt him, so shut the hell up and play."

He dealt the cards, and I looked from face to face, exaggerating flaws and reminding myself that these boys did not like me. The hope was that I might crush any surviving atom of attraction, but as has been the case for my entire life, the more someone dislikes me the more attractive he becomes. The key was to stall, to argue every hand until the sun came up and Mrs. Winters saved me with whatever cheerful monstrosity she'd planned for breakfast.

On the off chance that stalling would *not* work, I stepped into the bathroom and checked to make sure I was wearing clean underwear. A boner would be horrible beyond belief, but a boner combined with a skid mark meant that I should take the ketchup-smeared knife and just kill myself before it was too late.

"What are you, launching a sub in there?" Walt shouted. "Come on, we're waiting."

Usually when I was forced to compete, it

was my tactic to simply give up. To try in any way was to announce your ambition, which only made you more vulnerable. The person who wanted to win but failed was a loser, while the person who didn't really care was just a weirdo — a title I had learned to live with. Here, though, surrender was not an option. I had to win at a game I knew nothing about, and that seemed hopeless until I realized we were all on an equal footing. Not even Scott had the slightest idea what he was doing, and by feigning an air of expertise, I found I could manipulate things in my favor.

"A joker and a queen is much better than the four and five of spades," I said, defending my hand against Brad Clancy's.

"But you have a joker and a three of diamonds."

"Yes, but the joker *makes* it a queen."

"I thought you said that poker was against your religion," Walt said.

"Well, that doesn't mean I don't understand it. Greeks *invented* cards, remember. They're in my blood."

At the start of the game, the starburst clock had read three-thirty. An hour later I was missing one shoe, Scott and Brad had lost their shirts, and both Walt and Dale were down to their underwear. If this was what winning felt like, I wondered why I hadn't tried it before. Confidently in the lead, I invented little reasons for the undressed to get up and move about the room.

"Hey, Walt, did you hear that? It sounded like footsteps up in the kitchen."

"I didn't hear anything."

"Why don't you go to the stairway and check. We don't want any surprises." His underwear was all bunchy in the back, saggy like a diaper, but his legs were meaty and satisfying to look at.

"Dale, would you make sure those curtains are closed?"

He crossed the room, and I ate him alive with my eyes, confident that no one would accuse me of staring. Things might have been different were I in last place, but as a winner, it was my right to make sure that things were done properly. "There's an open space down by the baseboard. Bend over and close it, will you?"

It took a while, but after explaining that a pair of kings was no match for a two of hearts and a three of spades, Walt surrendered his underpants and tossed them onto a pile beside the TV set. "Okay," he said. "Now the rest of you can finish the game."

"But it *is* finished," Scott said.

"Oh no," Walt said. "I'm not the only

one getting naked. You guys have to keep playing."

"While you do what — sit back and *watch?*" I said. "What kind of a homo are you?"

"Yeah," Dale said. "Why don't we do something else? This game's boring and the rules are impossible."

The others muttered in agreement, and when Walt refused to back down, I gathered the deck and tamped it commandingly upon the tabletop. "The only solution is for us *all* to keep playing."

"How the hell do you expect me to do that?" Walt said. "In case you haven't noticed, there's nothing more for me to lose."

"Oh," I said, "there's always more. Maybe if the weakest hand is already naked, we should make that person perform some kind of a task. Nothing big, just, you know, a token kind of a thing."

"A thing like what?" Walt asked.

"I don't know. I guess we'll just have to cross that bridge when we come to it."

In retrospect, I probably went a little too far in ordering Scott to sit on my lap. "But I'm naked!" he said.

"Hey," I told him, "I'm the one who's going to be suffering. I was just looking for something easy. Would you rather run outside and touch the mailbox? The sun will be coming up in about twenty seconds — you want the whole neighborhood to see you?"

"How long will I have to sit on you?" he asked.

"I don't know. A minute or two. Maybe five. Or seven."

I moved onto the easy chair and wearily patted my knee, as if this were a great sacrifice. Scott slid into place, and I considered our reflection in the darkened TV screen. Here I was, one naked guy on my lap and three others ready to do my bidding. It was the stuff of dreams until I remembered that they were not doing these things of their own accord. This was not their pleasure, but their punishment, and once it was over they would make it a point to avoid me. Rumors would spread that I had slipped something into their Cokes, that I had tried to French Brad Clancy, that I had stolen five dollars from Walt's pocket. Not even Mrs. Winters would wave at me, but all that would come later, in a different life. For now I would savor this poor imitation of tenderness, mapping Scott's shoulders, the small of his back, as he shuddered beneath my winning hand.

Consider the Stars

Every night before going to bed, Hugh steps outside to consider the stars. His interest is not scientific — he doesn't pinpoint the constellations or make casual references to Canopus; rather, he just regards the mass of them, occasionally pausing to sigh. When asked if there's life on other planets, he says, "Yes, of course. Look at the odds."

It hardly seems fair we'd get the universe all to ourselves, but on a personal level I'm highly disturbed by the thought of extraterrestrial life. If there are, in fact, billions of other civilizations, where does that leave our celebrities? If worth is measured on a sliding scale of recognition, what would it mean if we were all suddenly obscure? How would we know our place?

In trying to make sense of this, I think back to a 1968 Labor Day celebration at the Raleigh Country Club. I was at the snack bar, listening to a group of sixth-graders who lived in another part of town and sat discussing significant changes in their upcoming school year. According to the girl named Janet, neither Pam Dobbins nor J. J. Jackson had been invited to the Fourth of July party hosted by the Duffy twins, who later told Kath Matthews that both Pam *and* J.J. were out of the picture as far as the seventh grade was concerned. "Totally, completely out," Janet said. "Poof."

I didn't know any Pam Dobbins or J. J. Jackson, but the reverential tone of Janet's voice sent me into a state of mild shock. Call me naive, but it had simply never occurred to me that other schools might have their own celebrity circles. At the age of twelve, I thought the group at E. C. Brooks was if not nationally known, then at least its own private phenomenon. Why else would our lives revolve around it so completely? I myself was not a member of my school's popular crowd, but I recall thinking that, whoever they were, Janet's popular crowd couldn't begin to compete with ours. But what if I was wrong? What if I'd wasted my entire life comparing myself with people who didn't really matter? Try as I might, I still can't wrap my mind around it.

They banded together in the third grade.

Ann Carlsworth, Christie Kaymore, Deb Bevins, Mike Holliwell, Doug Middleton, Thad Pope: they were the core of the popular crowd, and for the next six years my classmates and I studied their lives the way we were supposed to study math and English. What confused us most was the absence of any specific formula. Were they funny? No. Interesting? Yawn. None owned pools or horses. They had no special talents, and their grades were unremarkable. It was their dearth of excellence that gave the rest of us hope and kept us on our toes. Every now and then they'd select a new member, and the general attitude among the student body was "Oh, pick me!" It didn't matter what you were like on your own. The group would *make* you special. That was its magic.

So complete was their power that I actually felt honored when one of them hit me in the mouth with a rock. He'd gotten me after school, and upon returning home, I ran into my sister's bedroom, hugging my bloody Kleenex and crying, "It was Thad!!!"

Lisa was one grade higher than me, but still she understood the significance. "Did he *say* anything?" she asked. "Did you save the rock?"

My father demanded I retaliate, saying I ought to knock the guy on his ass.

"Oh, Dad."

"Aww, baloney. Clock him on the snot locker and he'll go down like a ton of bricks."

"Are you talking to *me?*" I asked. The archaic slang aside, who did my father think I was? Boys who spent their weekends making banana nut muffins did not, as a rule, excel in the art of hand-to-hand combat.

"I mean, come on, Dad," Lisa said. "Wake up."

The following afternoon I was taken to Dr. Povlitch for X-rays. The rock had damaged one of my bottom teeth, and there was some question over who would pay for the subsequent root canal. I figured that since my parents had conceived me, delivered me into the world, and raised me as a permanent guest in their home, they should foot the bill, but my father thought differently. He decided the Popes should pay, and I screamed as he picked up the phone book.

"But you can't just . . . *call* Thad's house."

"Oh yeah?" he said. "Watch me."

There were two Thad Popes in the Raleigh phone book, a Junior and a Senior. The one in my class was what came after a Junior. He was a Third. My father called both the Junior and the Senior, beginning each conversation with the line "Lou Sedaris here. Listen, pal, we've got a problem with your son."

He said our last name as if it meant something, as if we were known and respected. This made it all the more painful when he was asked to repeat it. Then to spell it.

A meeting was arranged for the following evening, and before we left the house, I begged my father to change his clothes. He'd been building an addition to the carport and was wearing a pair of khaki shorts smeared with paint and spotted here and there with bits of dried concrete. Through a hole in his tattered T-shirt, without squinting, it was possible to see his nipple.

"What the hell is wrong with this?" he asked. "We're not staying for dinner, so who cares what I'm wearing?"

I yelled for my mother, and in the end he compromised by changing his shirt.

From the outside, Thad's house didn't look much different from anyone else's —

61

just a standard split-level with what my father described as a totally inadequate carport. Mr. Pope answered the door in a pair of sherbet-colored golf pants and led us downstairs into what he called "the rumpus room."

"Oh," I said, "this is nice!"

The room was damp and windowless and lit with hanging Tiffany lampshades, the shards of colorful glass arranged to spell the words *Busch* and *Budweiser*. The walls were paneled in imitation walnut, and the furniture looked as though it had been hand-hewn by settlers who'd reconfigured parts of their beloved Conestoga wagon to fashion such things as easy chairs and coffee tables. Noticing the fraternity paddle hanging on the wall above the television, my father launched into his broken Greek, saying *"Kalispera sas adhelfos!"*

When Mr. Pope looked at him blankly, my father laughed and offered a translation. "I said, 'Good evening, brother.' "

"Oh . . . right," Mr. Pope said. "Fraternities are Greek."

He directed us toward a sofa and asked if we wanted something to drink. Coke? A beer? I didn't want to deplete Thad's precious cola supply, but before I could refuse, my father said sure, we'd have one of each. The orders were called up the staircase, and a few minutes later Mrs. Pope came down, carrying cans and plastic tumblers.

"Well, *hello* there," my father said. This was his standard greeting to a beautiful woman, but I could tell he was just saying it as a joke. Mrs. Pope wasn't unattractive, just ordinary, and as she set the drinks before us, I noticed that her son had inherited her blunt, slightly upturned nose, which looked good on him but caused her to appear overly suspicious and judgmental.

"So," she said. "I hear you've been to the dentist." She was just trying to make small talk, but because of her nose, it came off sounding like an insult, as if I'd just had a cavity filled and was now looking for someone to foot the bill.

"*I'll* say he's been to the dentist," my father said. "Someone hits you in the mouth with a rock and I'd say the dentist's office is pretty much the first place a reasonable person would go."

Mr. Pope held up his hands. "Whoa now," he said. "Let's just calm things down a little." He yelled upstairs for his son, and when there was no answer he picked up the phone, telling Thad to stop running his mouth and get his butt down to the rumpus room ASAP.

A rush of footsteps on the carpeted staircase and then Thad sprinted in, all smiles and apologies. The minister had called. The game had been rescheduled. "Hello, sir, and you are . . . ?"

He looked my father in the eye and firmly shook his hand, holding it in his own for just the right amount of time. While most handshakes mumbled, his spoke clearly, saying both *We'll get through this as quickly as possible* and *I'm looking forward to your vote this coming November.*

I'd thought that seeing him without his group might be unsettling, like finding a single arm on the sidewalk, but Thad was fully capable of operating independently. Watching him in action, I understood that his popularity was not an accident. Unlike a normal human being, he possessed an uncanny ability to please people. There was no sucking up or awkward maneuvering to fit the will of others. Rather, much like a Whitman's sampler, he seemed to offer a little bit of everything. Pass on his athletic ability and you might partake of his excellent manners, his confidence, his coltish enthusiasm. Even his parents seemed invigorated by his presence, uncrossing their legs and sitting up just a little bit straighter as he took a seat beside them. Had the circumstances been different, my father would have been all over him, probably going so far as to call him son — but money was involved, so he steeled himself.

"All right, then," Mr. Pope said. "Now that everyone's accounted for, I'm hoping we can clear this up. Sticks and stones aside, I suspect this all comes down to a little misunderstanding between friends."

I lowered my eyes, waiting for Thad to set his father straight. *"Friends? With him?"* I expected laughter or the famous Thad snort, but instead he said nothing. And with his silence, he won me completely. A little misunderstanding — that's *exactly* what it was. How had I not seen it earlier?

The immediate goal was to save my friend, and so I claimed to have essentially thrown myself in the path of Thad's fast-moving rock.

"What the hell was he throwing rocks for?" my father asked. "What the hell was he throwing them *at?*"

Mrs. Pope frowned, implying that such language was not welcome in the rumpus room.

"I mean, Jesus Christ, the guy's got to be a complete idiot."

Thad swore he hadn't been aiming at anything, and I backed him up, saying it was just one of those things we all did. "Like in Vietnam or whatever. It was just friendly fire."

My father asked what the hell I knew about Vietnam, and again Thad's mother winced, saying that boys picked up a lot of this talk by watching the news.

"You don't know what you're talking about," my father said.

"What my wife meant . . . ," Mr. Pope said.

"Aww, baloney."

The trio of Popes exchanged meaningful glances, holding what amounted to a brief, telepathic powwow. "This man crazy," the smoke signals read. "Make heap big trouble for others."

I looked at my father, a man in dirty shorts who drank his beer from the can rather than pouring it into his tumbler, and I thought, *You don't belong here.* More precisely, I decided that he was the reason *I* didn't belong. The hokey Greek phrases, the how-to lectures on mixing your own concrete, the squabble over who would pay the stupid dentist bill — little by little, it had all seeped into my bloodstream, robbing me of my natural ability to please others. For as long as I could remember, he'd been telling us that it didn't matter what other people thought: their judgment was crap, a waste of time, baloney. But it did matter, especially when those people were *these* people.

"Well," Mr. Pope said, "I can see that this is going nowhere."

My father laughed. "Yeah, you got that right." It sounded like a parting sentence, but rather than standing to leave, he leaned back in the sofa and rested his beer can upon his stomach. "We're all going nowhere."

At this point I'm fairly sure that Thad and I were envisioning the same grim scenario. While the rest of the world moved on, my increasingly filthy and bearded father would continue to occupy the rumpus-room sofa. Christmas would come, friends would visit, and the Popes would bitterly direct them toward the easy chairs. "Just ignore him," they'd say. "He'll go home sooner or later."

In the end, they agreed to pay for half of the root canal, not because they thought it was fair but because they wanted us out of their house.

★ ★ ★

Some friendships are formed by a commonality of interests and ideas: you both love judo or camping or making your own sausage. Other friendships are forged in alliance against a common enemy. On leaving Thad's house, I decided that ours would probably be the latter. We'd start off grousing about my father, and then, little by little, we'd move on to the hundreds of other things and people that got on our nerves. "You hate olives," I imagined him saying. "I hate them, too!"

As it turned out, the one thing we both hated was me. Rather, I hated me. Thad couldn't even summon up the enthusiasm. The day after the meeting, I approached him in the lunchroom, where he sat at his regular table, surrounded by his regular friends. "Listen," I said, "I'm really sorry about that stuff with my dad." I'd worked up a whole long speech, complete with imitations, but by the time I finished my mission statement, he'd turned to resume his conversation with Doug Middleton. Our perjured testimony, my father's behavior, even the rock throwing: I was so far beneath him that it hadn't even registered.

Poof.

The socialites of E. C. Brooks shone even brighter in junior high, but come tenth grade, things began to change. Desegregation drove a lot of the popular people into private schools, and those who remained seemed silly and archaic, deposed royalty from a country the average citizen had ceased to care about.

Early in our junior year, Thad was jumped by a group of the new black kids, who yanked off his shoes and threw them in the toilet. I knew I was supposed to be happy, but part of me felt personally assaulted. True, he'd been a negligent prince, yet still I believed in the monarchy. When his name was called at graduation, it was I who clapped the longest, outlasting even his parents, who politely stopped once he'd left the stage.

I thought about Thad a lot over the coming years, wondering where he went to college and if he joined a fraternity. The era of the Big Man on Campus had ended, but the rowdy houses with their pool tables and fake moms continued to serve as reunion points for the once popular, who were now viewed as date rapists and budding alcoholics. I tell myself that while his brothers drifted toward a confused and bitter adulthood, Thad stumbled into the class that changed his life. He's the poet laureate of Liechtenstein, the surgeon who cures cancer with love, the ninth-grade teacher who insists that the world is big enough for everyone. When moving to another city, I'm always hoping to find him living in the apartment next door. We'll meet in the hallway and he'll stick out his hand, saying, "Excuse me, but don't I — *shouldn't* I know you?" It doesn't have to happen today, but it *does* have to happen. I've kept a space waiting for him, and if he doesn't show up, I'm going to have to forgive my father.

The root canal that was supposed to last for ten years has now lasted for over thirty, though it's nothing to be proud of. Having progressively dulled and weakened, the tooth is now a brownish gray color the Conran's catalog refers to as "Kabuki." It's hanging in there, but just barely. While Dr. Povlitch worked out of a converted brick house beside the Colony Shopping Center, my current dentist, Docteur Guig, has an office near the Madeleine, in Paris. On a recent visit, he gripped my dead tooth between his fingertips and gently jiggled it back and forth. I hate to unnecessarily exhaust his patience, so when he asked me what had happened, it took me a moment to think of the clearest possible answer. The past was far too complicated to put into French, so instead I envisioned a perfect future, and attributed the root canal to a little misunderstanding between friends.

Monie Changes Everything

My mother had a great-aunt who lived outside of Cleveland and visited us once in Binghamton, New York. I was six years old but can clearly remember her car moving up the newly paved driveway. It was a silver Cadillac driven by a man in a flattopped cap, the kind worn by policemen. He opened the back door with great ceremony, as if this were a coach, and we caught sight of the great-aunt's shoes, which were orthopedic yet fancy, elaborately tooled leather with little heels the size of spools. The shoes were followed by the hem of a mink coat, the tip of a cane, and then, finally, the great-aunt herself, who was great because she was rich and childless.

"Oh, Aunt Mildred," my mother said, and we looked at her strangely. In private she referred to her as "Aunt Monie," a cross between *moaning* and *money*, and the proper name was new to us.

"Sharon!" Aunt Monie said. She looked at our father, and then at us.

"This is my husband, Lou," my mother said. "And these are our children."

"How nice. Your children."

The driver handed my father several shopping bags and then returned to the car as the rest of us stepped inside.

"Would he like to use the bathroom or something?" my mother whispered. "I mean, he's more than welcome to. . . ."

Aunt Monie laughed, as if my mother had asked if the car itself would like to come indoors. "Oh, no, dear. He'll stay outside."

I don't believe my father gave her a tour, the way he did with most visitors. He had designed parts of the house himself, and enjoyed describing what they might have looked like had he not intervened. "What I've done," he'd say, "is put the barbecue pit right here in the kitchen, where it'll be closer to the refrigerator." The guests would congratulate him on his ingenuity, and then he would lead them into the breakfast nook. I hadn't been in too many houses but understood that ours was very nice. The living-room window overlooked the backyard and, beyond that, a deep forest. In the winter deer came and tiptoed around the bird feeder, ignoring the meat scraps my sisters and I had neatly arranged for their dining pleasure. Even without the snow, the view was impressive, but Aunt Monie seemed not to notice it. The only thing she commented on was the living-room sofa, which was gold and seemed to amuse her. "My goodness," she said to my four-year-old sister, Gretchen. "Did you choose this yourself?" Her smile was brief and amateurish, like something she was studying but had not yet mastered. The mouth turned up at the corners, but her eyes failed to follow. Rather than sparkling, they remained flat and impassive, like old dimes.

"All right then," she said. "Let's see what we've got." She received my sisters and me, each in turn, and handed us an unwrapped present from an exotic shopping bag at her feet. The bag was from a Cleveland department store, a store that for many years had been hers, or at least partially. Her first husband had owned it, and when he died she had married a tool-and-die manufacturer who eventually sold his business to Black and Decker. He, too, had passed away, and she had inherited everything.

My gift was a marionette. Not the cheap kind with a blurred plastic face, but a wooden one, each fine joint attached by hook to a black string. "This is Pinocchio," Aunt Monie said. "His nose is long from telling lies. Is that something *you* like to do from time to time, tell little lies?" I started to answer, and she turned to my sister Lisa. "And who have we here?" It was like visiting Santa, or rather, like having him visit you. She gave us each an expensive gift, and then she went to the bathroom to powder her nose. With most people this was just an expression, but when she returned, her face was matted, as if with flour, and she smelled strongly of roses. My mother asked her to stay for lunch, and Aunt Monie explained that it was impossible. "What with Hank," she said, "the long drive, I just couldn't." Hank, we figured, was the chauffeur, who raced to open the car door the moment we stepped out of the house. Our great-aunt settled into the backseat and covered her lap with a fur blanket. "You can close the door now," she said, and we stood in the driveway, my marionette waving a tangled good-bye.

I hoped Aunt Monie might become a fixture, but she never visited again. A few times a year, most often on a Sunday afternoon, she would phone the house and ask for my mother. The two of them would talk for fifteen minutes or so, but it never seemed joyful, the way it did when my regular aunt called. Rather than laughing and using her free hand to roll her hair, my mother would compress a length of phone cord, holding it in her fist like a stack of coins. "Aunt Mildred!" she'd say. "How perfectly nice to hear from you." Lean in to listen and she'd use her bare foot to push you away. "Nothing. I was just sitting here, looking out at the bird feeder. You like birds, don't you? . . . No? Well, to tell you the truth, neither do I. Lou thinks they're interesting but . . . exactly. Give them an inch and they'll take a mile."

It was like seeing her naked.

When I went to camp in Greece it was Aunt Monie who bought my ticket. It seems unlikely that she would have called specifically asking how she might brighten my life, so I imagine that my mother must have mentioned it, the way you do when you're hoping the other person might offer a hand. "Lisa's going but what with the cost, I'm afraid that David will just have to wait a few years. You what? Oh, Aunt Mildred, I couldn't."

But she could.

We learned that every night Aunt Monie ate a lamb chop for dinner. Every year she bought a new Cadillac. "Can you beat that?" my father said. "Puts maybe two thousand miles on it and then she runs out and gets another one. Probably pays full sticker price, if I know her." It struck him as insane, but to the rest of us it was the very definition of class. This was what money bought: the freedom to shop without dicking for discounts and low-interest payment plans. My father replaced the station wagon and it took him months, hectoring the salesmen until they'd do anything to get rid of him. He demanded and received an extended lifetime warranty on the refrigerator, meaning, I guessed, that should it leak in the year 2020, he'd return from the grave and trade it in. Money to him meant individual dollars, slowly accumulating like drips from a spigot. To Aunt Monie it seemed more like an ocean. Spend a wave and before they could draw up a receipt, there was another one crashing onto the shore. This was the beauty of dividends.

In return for my trip to Greek camp, my mother demanded that I write her aunt a thank-you letter. It wasn't much to ask, but try as I might, I could never get beyond the first sentence. I wanted to convince Aunt Monie that I was better than the rest of my family, that I *understood* a sticker-price Cadillac and a diet of lamb chops, but how to begin? I thought of my mother, flip-flopping on the topic of birds. On the phone you could backpedal and twist yourself to suit the other person's opinions, but it was much harder in a letter, where your words were set in stone.

"~~Dear Aunt Mildred~~." "My Dearest Aunt Mildred." I wrote that Greece was great, and then I erased it, announcing that Greece was okay. This, I worried, might make me seem ungrateful, and so I started over. "Greece is ancient" seemed all right until I realized that, at the age of eighty-six, she was not much younger than the Temple of Delphi. "Greece is poor," I wrote. "Greece is hot." "Greece is interesting but probably not as interesting as Switzerland." After ten tries I gave up. On returning to Raleigh, my mother took one of my souvenirs, a salt sculpture of a naked discus thrower, and mailed it off with a note she'd forced me to write at the kitchen table. "Dear Aunt Mildred. Thanks a lot!" It hardly established me as a diamond in the rough, but I told myself I'd send a proper letter the following week. The following week I put it off again, and on and on until it was too late.

★ ★ ★

A few months after my trip to Greece my mother, her sister, and their homosexual cousin visited Aunt Monie at her home in Gates Mills. I had heard about this cousin, favorably from my mother and despairingly from my father, who liked to relate the following story. "A group of us went to South Carolina. It was me, your mother, Joyce and Dick, and this cousin, this Philip, right. So we go for a swim in the ocean and . . ." At this point he would start to laugh. "We go for a swim and when we get back to the hotel Philip knocks on the door, asking if he can borrow, get this, asking if he can borrow your mother's *hair dryer.*" That was it. End of story. He didn't stick it up his ass or anything, just used it in the traditional manner, but still my father found it incredible. "I mean, a hair dryer! Can you beat that!"

I was obsessed with Philip, who managed a college library somewhere in the Midwest. "He's a lot like you," my mother would say. "A big reader. Loves books." I was not a big reader but had managed to convince her otherwise. When asked what I'd been up to all afternoon, I never said, "Oh, masturbating," or, "Imagining what my room might look like painted scarlet."

79

I'd say that I'd been reading, and she fell for it every time. Never asked the name of the book, never asked where I'd gotten it, just, "Oh, that's nice."

Because they lived in the same part of the country, Philip saw a lot of Aunt Monie. The two of them went on occasional vacations, sometimes alone and sometimes in the company of Philip's *friend,* a word my mother said in italics, not in a bad way, but like a wink, suggesting that the term had more than one meaning and that this second meaning was a lot more interesting than the first. "They have a lovely house," my mother said. "It's on a lake and they're thinking of getting a boat."

"I *bet* they are," my father said, and then he repeated the story of the hair dryer. "Can you beat that! A man wanting to use a hair dryer."

Philip and Aunt Monie shared a taste for the finer things: the symphony, the opera, clear soups. Theirs was a relationship enjoyed by the childless, sophisticated adults who could finish a sentence without being hounded for a ride to the Kwik Pik or an advance on next year's allowance. Resenting my mother for having children put me in a difficult position, and so I wished she had just had one, me, and that we lived outside of Cleveland. We needed to ingratiate ourselves and be close at hand when Aunt Monie took to her death bed, which could, I figured, happen any day. Aunt Joyce was now flying to Ohio three times a year and would phone my mother with updates. She reported that walking had become difficult, that Hank had installed one of those contraptions that slowly hoisted a chair up and down the stairs, that Mildred had become "I guess the best word is *paranoid*," she said.

When Aunt Monie could no longer finish an entire lamb chop, my mother made plans for a visit of her own. I thought she'd go with her sister or homosexual Philip, but instead she took Lisa and me. We went for a three-day weekend in mid-October. Aunt Monie's driver met us at the baggage carousel and led us outside to the waiting Cadillac. "Oh, please," my mother said as he ushered her toward the backseat. "I'm sitting up front and I don't want to hear another word about it."

Hank moved to open the door but she beat him to it. "And don't give me that 'Mrs. Sedaris' business, either. The name's Sharon, got it?" She was the sort of person who could talk to anyone, not in the pointed, investigative manner that the situation called for, but generally, casually. Had she been sent to interview Charles Manson, she might have come away saying, "I never knew he liked bamboo!" It was maddening.

We left the airport and passed into a wasteland. Men stood on rusty bridges, watching as filthy trains coupled on the tracks below. Black clouds issued from smokestacks as Hank detailed his method for curing hams. I'd wanted to hear what it was like working for Aunt Monie, but my mother never led him in that direction. "Hams!" she said. "Now you're talking my language."

The landscape gradually softened, and by the time we reached Gates Mills the world was beautiful. Here were brilliant thick-trunked trees surrounding homes made of stone and painted brick. A couple dressed in bright red jackets rode a pair of horses down the middle of the street, and Hank passed slowly to avoid spooking them. This was, he explained, a suburb, and I thought he must be using the wrong word. Suburbs meant wooden houses, the streets named after the wives and girlfriends of the developer: Laura Drive, Kimberly Circle, Nancy Ann Cul-de-Sac.

Where were the boats and campers, the mailboxes done up to look like caves or bank vaults or igloos?

"Stop . . . *now*," I whispered as the car passed a slightly smaller version of Windsor Castle. "Stop . . . *now*." The fear was that we'd drive beyond the ostentation and wind up in a plain neighborhood resembling our own. Hank kept going and I worried that Aunt Monie was one of those guilt-ridden rich people you sometimes read about, the kind who volunteered in burn units and tried not to draw too much attention to themselves. The conversation had moved from hams to sausages and was testing the waters of barbecue when the Cadillac turned toward what was unquestionably the finest home of all. It was the sort of place you'd see on the cover of a college catalog: the Deanery, the Hall of Great Fellows. Ivy hugged the stone walls, and windowpanes the size of playing cards glinted in the sun. Even the air smelled rich, the scent of decaying leaves tinged with what I imagined to be myrrh. There was no maze or pond-size fountain, but the lawn was well tended and included a second, smaller house Hank referred to as "the outbuilding." He gathered our bags from the trunk, and as we waited, the equestrians passed the front of the house, tipping their velvet hats in salute. "Do you hear that?" my mother asked. She clasped her collar tight against her throat. "Don't you just love the sound of hooves?"

We did.

A maid named Dorothy stepped out to greet us, and as if my sister were blind and unable to take in such wonders on her own, I turned and whispered, "She's white. And she's wearing a *uniform.*"

The maids in Raleigh might wear pant-suits or cast-off nursing smocks, but this was the real thing: the starched black dress trimmed in white at the cuffs and collar. She wore an apron as well, and an unflattering cap, which sat on her head like a tiny cushion.

While regular maids mumbled, Dorothy announced. "Mrs. Brown is resting." "Mrs. Brown will be down presently." Like a talking doll, her side of the conversation seemed limited to a handful of prerecorded statements. "Yes, ma'am," "No, ma'am," "I'll have the car brought round to the door." While waiting, we ate sandwiches of smoked salmon served with potato salad. I suggested that we nose around, or at least move beyond the kitchen, but the idea proved unpopular. "Mrs. Brown is resting," Dorothy said. "Mrs. Brown will be down presently." It was nearly dusk when Aunt Monie telephoned the kitchen, and we were allowed to enter the main parlor.

"How'd you like to dust *this*," my mother said, and I shuddered at her lack of sophistication. The whole point of finery was that someone *else* handled the upkeep, polishing the end tables and reaming crud from between the toes of lion-paw easy chairs. That said, I'd have hated to dust it. A lampshade or two would have been all right, but this resembled one of those period rooms cordoned off at the museum, the furniture gathered in tight little cliques like guests at a party. Walls were papered in satin stripes, and curtains fell from floor to ceiling, bordered by what were later identified as swags. The potty-chair and folding card table didn't quite fit in, but those we pretended not to notice.

"Mrs. Brown," Dorothy announced, and we followed the noise of the grinding gears, gathering before the newel post to stare up at the approaching chair. The Aunt Monie I'd met ten years earlier had been rickety but substantial enough to leave a dent in the sofa cushion. The one that now droned down the staircase seemed to weigh no more than a puppy.

She was still elegantly dressed, but withered, her balding head drooping from her shoulders like an old onion. My mother identified herself, and once the chair had settled onto firm ground, Aunt Monie stared at her for a few moments.

"It's Sharon," my mother repeated. "And these are two of my children. My daughter Lisa and my son David."

"Your children?"

"Well, some of my children," my mother said. "The oldest two."

"And you are?"

"Sharon."

"Sharon, right."

"You sent me to Greece a few years ago," I said. "Remember that? You paid for my trip and I sent you all those letters."

"Yes," she said. "Letters."

"Very long letters."

"Very long."

The guilt I'd stored was suddenly gone, replaced by the fear that she'd forgotten to mention us in her will. What was going on in that wispy head of hers? *Mom,* I whispered. *Make her remember who we are.*

As it turned out, Aunt Monie was a lot sharper than she appeared. Names weren't her strong suit, but she was incredibly perceptive, at least as far as I was concerned.

"Where's that boy," she'd ask my mother whenever I left the room. "Call him back here. I don't like people snooping through my things."

"Oh, I'm sure he's not snooping," my mother would say. "Lisa, go find your brother."

Aunt Monie's second husband had been a big-game hunter, and off the main parlor he'd built a grand trophy room, a virtual ark of taxidermy. The big-cat corner included snow leopards, white tigers, a lion, and a pair of panthers mounted in midleap. Mountain goats butted horns before the coffee table. A wolverine stalked a doe from behind the sofa, while beside the gun case a grizzly bear raised her Bunyanesque paw, protecting the cub that cowered between her knees. There were the animals, and there were the objects made from animals: an elephant-foot stool, cloven ashtrays, the leg of a giraffe turned into a standing lamp. *How'd you like to dust this!*

I first entered the room during one of Aunt Monie's baths, taking a seat on a zebra-skin ottoman and experiencing the dual sensations of envy and paranoia: a thousand eyes watching, and I wanted every one of them. If forced to choose, I'd have taken the gorilla, but according to my mother, the entire collection had been willed to a small natural history museum somewhere in Canada. I asked what Canada needed with another moose, but she just shrugged and told me I was morbid.

When expelled from the trophy room, I'd go outside and stare at it through the windows. "Where is he?" Aunt Monie would ask. "What's he up to?"

Early one evening, after staring through the trophy-room window, I moved among the shrubs and watched as Mrs. Brightleaf, the part-time nurse, dissected Aunt Monie's lamb chop. The two of them were seated at the folding card table, overlooked by a portrait of husband number two, who knelt on a felled rhinoceros. My mother entered from the kitchen, and I was startled by how out of place she looked, how wrong amid the hired help and scalloped end tables. I'd always assumed that given a full set of teeth, a person could step from one class to another, moving effortlessly from the ranch house to the manor, but it now seemed that I was wrong. A life like Aunt Monie's required not just study but a certain proclivity for pretension, something not all of us were blessed with. My mother waved her highball glass, and when she jokingly took a seat on the old woman's potty stool, I saw that we were doomed.

On Sunday afternoon Hank drove us back to the airport. Aunt Monie continued her downward spiral and died at home on the first day of spring. My parents attended the funeral and returned to Cleveland a few months later. There was, they said, the estate to settle, lawyers to meet, loose ends. They left Raleigh on a plane and returned a week later in the silver Cadillac, the fur blanket raising heat welts on my mother's knees. It seemed that she *had* been remembered — and fondly, too — but nothing would persuade her to reveal the exact amount.

"I'll give you a figure and you just point up or down," I said. "Was it a million dollars?"

"I'm not telling you."

"A million and a half?"

I gently prodded her in the middle of the night, hoping she might talk in her sleep. "Was it two million dollars? Seven hundred thousand?"

"I'm not telling you."

A friend phoned, pretending to be an IRS agent, but my mother saw right through it. Tax officials rarely had Jethro Tull records playing in the background. They also, apparently, never called saying, "I just have one quick question."

"But I have to know so that I can tell people."

"That's why I'm not telling you," my mother said.

I was working in a cafeteria then but still honored a once-a-week babysitting job I'd held since junior high. The children despised me, but there was a familiarity, almost a comfort, in their hatred, and so their parents kept me on. The family always had expensive food in their refrigerator: deli-sliced meats and cheeses. Bottles of artichoke hearts. One night as I was being paid, I told the wife that my great-aunt had died and that we now had a Cadillac and a fur lap blanket. "There's money, too," I said. "A lot of it." I thought the woman might welcome me into the fine-refrigerator club, but instead she rolled her eyes. "A Cadillac," she said. "My God, how nouveau riche can you get."

I wasn't sure what *nouveau riche* meant, but it didn't sound good. "That little bitch," my mother said when I repeated the story, and then she turned on me for having told the woman in the first place. A week later the Cadillac was gone, sold. I blamed myself, but it turned out my parents had been planning to get rid of it anyway. My mother bought herself a few nice suits. She stocked the refrigerator with cold cuts from the deli counter, but she did not buy a diamond or a beach house or any of the other things we expected of her. For a while the money was used as a bargaining chip. She and my father would argue over some little thing, and when he laughed and walked out of the room — which was how he always ended an argument, behaving as though you were crazy and nothing more could be said — my mother would shout, "You think I can't afford to leave? Just try me, buddy." If a neighbor treated her badly or someone in a shop acted as though she didn't exist, she'd return home and pound on the countertop, hissing, "I could buy and sell that son of a bitch." She had often imagined saying these words, and now that she could, I sensed she was disappointed by how little pleasure they brought.

I think it was Aunt Monie's money that paid my rent when I moved to Chicago to attend the Art Institute. I think it was her money that sent my sister Gretchen to the Rhode Island School of Design and sent my sister Tiffany to a horrible but very expensive reform school in Maine. It went toward getting my mother's children out of the South, which, for her, spelled improvement. The rest of the money was managed by my father, a financial alchemist who turned gold into a mailbox of annual reports that only he could enjoy.

As for the taxidermy, the Canadian museum declined my great-uncle's collection. It seemed too morose to auction off, and so the animals, along with the knickknacks made of their parts, were given to Hank.

"You *what?*" I said to my mother. "Let me get this straight. You *what?*" A phone call was made and I was sent a bearskin rug, which for several years sprawled on the floor of my too-small bedroom. It was a crazy thing to make a rug out of, really. Walk one way and you tripped over the head. Walk the other and you caught your foot in the open mouth.

Alone with my bear on the very first night, I double-locked the door and lay upon it naked, the way people sometimes did in magazines. I'd hoped this might be the best feeling in the world, the conquered fur against my bare flesh, but my only sensation was a creeping uneasiness. Someone was watching me, not a neighbor or one of my sisters, but Aunt Monie's second husband, the one I had seen in the portrait. From the neck up he closely resembled Teddy Roosevelt, the wire-rimmed glasses glinting above a disfiguring walrus mustache. The man had stalked wildebeest across the sizzling veldt and now his predatory eye fell upon me: an out-of-shape seventeen-year-old with over-size glasses and a turquoise-studded bracelet, cheapening the name of big-game hunting with his scrawny, pimpled butt. It was an unpleasant image, and so it stayed with me for a long, long time.

In her sophomore year of college Lisa took the rug to Virginia, where it loafed on the floor of her dorm room. It was, we'd agreed, a loan, but at the end of the spring term she gave it to her roommate, who died in a car accident while driving home to Pennsylvania. On hearing the news, I imagined her parents, this couple in their mind-boggling grief, coming upon the bear in the trunk of their daughter's car and wondering what it had to do with her, or anybody's, life.

The Change in Me

You know you're young when someone asks you for money and you take it as a compliment.

"You look pretty cool, can I ask you a question?"

The beggar was a girl in her late teens, a hippie standing outside the convenience store at the North Hills shopping center. She wore a peasant blouse and long, elephant-belled jeans that made it appear as though she had no feet. Granny glasses, amulets, a beaded headband: I couldn't believe that someone so sophisticated was actually talking to *me*.

I was thirteen that summer and had ridden to the Kwik Pik with my mother, who handed me a ten-dollar bill and asked me to run in for a carton of cigarettes. She watched the hippie ask me a question, watched me run into the store, and watched me stop on the way out to hand the girl a dollar.

"What was that?" she asked when I got

back into the car. "Who was that girl?" Had I been with my father, I would have lied, saying she was a friend, but my mother knew I had no interesting friends, and so I told the truth.

"You didn't give her *a* dollar," she said. "You gave her *my* dollar."

"But she needed it."

"What for?" my mother said. "Shampoo? A needle and thread?"

"I don't know. I didn't ask."

"I don't know. I didn't ask." Being mocked by the untalented was easy to brush off, but my mother was really good at imitating people. Coming from her, I sounded spoiled and vacant, like a Persian cat, only human. "If you want to give her a dollar, that's your own business," she said. "But that dollar was mine, and I want it back."

I offered to pay her when we got home, but that wasn't good enough. "I don't want just any old dollar," she said, "I want *that* one."

It was ridiculous to claim an attachment to a particular dollar bill, but for my mother this had become a matter of principle. "It's my dollar and I want it back."

When I told her it was too late, she got out and opened my car door. "Well, we'll just see about that," she said.

The hippie looked over in our direction, and I lowered myself in the seat. "Mom, please. You can't do this." It was touch-and-go for a moment, but I knew she'd stop short of actually dragging me from the station wagon. "Can't we put this behind us? I'll pay you back when we get home. Really, I swear."

She watched me cower and then she got back into the driver's seat. "You think everyone who asks for money actually needs it? God, are you gullible."

The spare-change girl seemed to have started a trend. On my next trip to the Kwik Pik I was hit up by another hippie — this one a guy — who squatted on the ground in front of the ice machine. He saw me approach and held out his leather hat. "Greetings, brother," he said. "Think you could manage to help a friend?"

I handed over the fifty cents I'd planned to spend on Coke and potato chips, and then I leaned against a post, watching this hippie and studying his ways. Some people, the cool people who had no extra money, made it a point to say, "Sorry, man," or "You know how it is." The hippie would nod, as if to familiar music, and the

cool person would do the same. The uncool people passed without stopping, but
still you could see that the hippie held a
strange power over them. "Spare change?
A dime? A quarter?" It was a small amount
that asked a big question: "Care ye not
about your fellow man?" It helped, I
thought, that he bore such a striking resemblance to Jesus, who was rumored to
be returning any day now.

I watched for half an hour, and then the
cashier came out, fluttering his hands as if
they were whisk brooms. "We can't have
you hassling the customers," he said. "Go
on, now. Scoot."

Hassle was a young person's word, and
coming from a full-grown man, it sounded
goofy, reminding me of the way movie
cowboys used the word *amigo*. I wanted the
hippie to stand up for himself, to say,
"Cool it, Baldie," or "Who's hassling
who?" but instead he just shrugged. It was
almost elegant, the way he picked himself
up off the ground and crossed the parking
lot to what was most likely his parents' car.
It didn't matter that he probably lived at
home, criticizing the system during the day
and sleeping each night in a comfortable
bed. He'd maybe put my quarters toward
some luxury — incense maybe, or guitar

strings — but that was no big deal, either. He was a grown-up's worst nightmare, and, minus the hat, I wanted to be just like him.

At that point in my life I was still receiving an allowance, three dollars a week, which I supplemented with babysitting and an occasional job at the Dorton Arena, a concert and exhibit hall located on the state fairgrounds. When we were lucky, my friend Dan and I wore white jackets and folding paper hats and worked the concessions counter. When, far more frequently, we were *un*lucky, we wore the same dopey outfits, hung heavy trays around our necks, and marched up and down the aisles, selling popcorn, peanuts, and the watered-down Cokes we were instructed to refer to as "ice-cold drinks."

In real life nobody said things like "ice-cold drinks," but our boss, Jerry, insisted on it. Worse than simply saying it, we had to shout it, which made me feel like a peddler or an old-time paperboy. During heavy-metal concerts we went unnoticed, but at the country-music shows — jamborees, they were called — people tended to complain when we barked through their favorite songs. "Stand by Your POPCORN,

PEANUTS, ICE-COLD DRINKS," "My Woman, My Woman, My POPCORN, PEANUTS, ICE-COLD DRINKS!" "Folsom Prison POPCORN, PEANUTS, ICE-COLD DRINKS." The angrier fans stormed downstairs to take it up with Jerry, who said, "Tough tittie. I got a business to run." He dismissed the complainers as "a bunch of tightwadded rednecks," which surprised me, as he was something of a redneck himself. The expression *tightwadded* was a pretty good indicator, as was his crew cut and the asthma inhaler he'd decorated with a tiny American flag.

"Maybe he means 'redneck' in an affectionate way," my mother said, but I didn't buy it. Far more likely he saw a difference between himself and the people who looked and acted just like him. I did this as well, and listening to Jerry made me realize how pathetic it sounded. Who was I to call someone uncool — me with the braces and thick black-framed glasses. "Oh, you look fine," my mother would say. She meant to reassure me, but looking fine to your mother meant that something was definitely wrong. I wanted to turn her stomach, but for the time being my hands were tied. According to the rules, I wasn't allowed to grow my hair out until I turned sixteen, the same age at which my sisters could finally pierce their ears. To my parents this made sense, but ears were pierced in a matter of minutes, while it took years to cultivate a decent ponytail. As it was, it would take me a good nine months just to catch up with Dan, whose mother was reasonable and did not hamper his style with senseless age restrictions. His hair was thick and straight and parted in the middle, the honey-colored hanks pushed behind his ears and falling to his shoulders like a set of well-hung curtains.

Ever since the fourth grade we had been mutual outcasts — the nature lovers, the spazzes — but with his new look Dan was pulling ahead, meeting cool people at his private school and going to their homes to listen to records. Now when I called somebody an L7 he looked at me the way that I had looked at Jerry — *cuckoo cuckoo* — and I understood that our friendship was coming to an end. Guys weren't supposed to be hurt by things like that, and so instead I settled into a quiet jealousy, which grew increasingly difficult to hide.

The state fair arrived in mid-September, and the concessions crew moved back and forth between concerts at the arena and smaller events held at the speedway. Dan and I were setting up for the first stock-car race when Jerry announced that instead of Coke, we'd be selling cans of something called Near Beer.

What separated near beer from the real thing was alcohol content. Beer had one, and Near Beer didn't. It tasted like carbonated oatmeal, but Jerry hoped the customers might be deceived by the label, which was robust and boozy-looking. "The mind can play tricks," he said.

Maybe he was right, but the minds that mistook a sugar tablet for an aspirin were not the minds that gathered to witness a North Carolina stock-car race. Our first load sold instantly, but come our second time out, people had begun to catch on. "Beer, my ass," they shouted. "Ya'lls is *deceivers.*"

"It'll pick up when the heat kicks in," Jerry said, but no one believed him.

There was an hourlong break between the first and second stock-car event, and as Dan and I walked along the midway I thought about a suede vest I'd seen the previous week at J. C. Penney's. It was what the saleswoman described as "a masculine cherry red," with lines of fringe swaying like bangs from the yoke. Eighteen dollars was a lot of money, but a vest like that would not go unnoticed. Couple it with a turtleneck or the right button-down shirt and it announced that you were sensitive and no stranger to peace. Wear it bare-chested and it suggested that, long hair or not, yours was a life lived in that devil-may-care region best described as "out there." I'd hoped that by working all weekend, I might earn enough to buy it, but what with the Near Beer, that was pretty much out of the question. Now I'd have to put it on my Christmas list, which definitely neutered the allure. What had seemed hip and dangerous would appear just the opposite when wrapped in a box marked "From Santa."

The bleachers were filling up for the second race, and as we headed back to the speedway I noticed a pair of squarely dressed boys staring up at the Ferris wheel. They looked like me, but a bit younger, brothers probably, wearing identical black-framed glasses secured to their heads with tight elastic bands. I saw them looking upward with their mouths open, and in that instant I saw my red suede vest.

"Spare change?"

The brothers looked at each other, and

then back at me. "Okay, sure," the older one said. "Gene, give this guy some money."

"Why do *I* have to?" Gene asked.

"Because I said so, that's why." The older brother unstrapped his glasses and rubbed a raw spot on the bridge of his nose. "You're a hippie, right?" He spoke as if, like Canadians or Methodists, hippies walked quietly among us, indistinguishable to the naked eye.

"Well, course he's a hippie," Gene said. "Otherwise, he wouldn't be bothering people." He sorted through his change and handed me a dime.

"Right on," I said.

It was the easiest thing in the world. Dan worked one side of the Ferris wheel, and I took the other. We asked for money the way you might ask for the time, and when someone gave it we blessed them with a peace sign or the squinty nod that translated to "I'm glad you know where I'm coming from." Adults were cheap, and too judgmental, so we stuck to people our own age, concentrating on the obvious out-of-towners who had heard about hippies but had never seen one in real life. People either gave or they didn't, but no one asked what we needed the money for or why two seemingly healthy teenagers would trouble complete strangers for change.

This was freedom, and to make it taste just that much sweeter, we worked our way back to the speedway, where Jerry was setting up for the third stock-car race. "I ought to kick ya'll's asses," he said. "Walking out on me the way you done, that's no way to treat a friend." He handed us our uniforms, and we tossed them on the counter, announcing that we'd found an easier way to make money.

"Then get on out of here," he said. "And don't come crawling back, neither. I don't have no use for backstabbers."

We had a high time with that one. Reminded of just how stupid a person looked in a paper hat, Dan and I returned to our panhandling, pausing every so often to tap each other on the shoulder. "Backstabber, you might think I've got some use for you, but think again." As the afternoon moved on, we replaced the word *backstabber* with the word *hippie*, allowing ourselves to believe that Jerry had fired us not because we had walked out on him but because we were free and of the moment. It didn't matter that we'd never work for him again, as those days were behind us now. Work was behind us.

By five o'clock I had begged enough money to pay for my vest, but Dan and I were greedy and not ready to stop. Plans were made for stereo systems and minibikes, anything we wanted, paid for in dimes. Dusk approached and the midway brightened with colored bulbs. The early evening was lucrative, but then a different crowd swept through and the mood became rowdy.

"Spare change?"

The guy I'd approached had a downy, immature mustache, no more than a few dozen hairs positioned above a mouth the size of a newborn baby's.

"What did you say?" he asked.

I turned away, and when he spun me back around to face him, I noticed his army jacket, which wasn't the old ironic kind but a crisp new one, the type you'd buy as practice before you enlisted.

"Did you talk to me, weirdo?" His mouth was bigger now. "Did you say something to my face?"

A second boy stepped up and put his hand on the angry guy's shoulder. "Come on, Kurt," he said. "Take it easy."

"Maybe you don't understand what's going on," the guy named Kurt said, "but this bozo talked to me." He spoke with great outrage, as if I'd peed in his mouth. "I mean, he actually *said* something *to* me."

Two of their friends who had walked ahead came back to see what the fuss was about and stood with their arms crossed as Kurt explained the situation. "I was minding my own business and this piece of shit started running his mouth. Comes right up as if he knows me, but he doesn't *know* me. Nobody fucking *knows* me."

The only thing worse than a twenty-five-year-old with a Vietnam flashback was a fourteen-year-old with a Vietnam flash-forward. I turned my head to look for Dan and saw him backing away just as Kurt's fist caught my ear, breaking the stem off my glasses and sending them to the ground. The second punch grazed my upper lip, and the third was interrupted by the friends, who grabbed Kurt by the arms, saying, "Hey, man, take it easy. He's not worth it."

I tasted the blood leaking from my lip. "It's true," I said. "I'm not worth it. I swear I'm not. You can ask anyone."

"He shouldn't go talking to people when he doesn't know who the fuck he's talking to," Kurt said. "The next time someone gets in my face, I'll fucking kill him. I swear I will."

"We know, buddy. We know." Kurt's friends led him down the midway, and a minute later one of them returned to hand me a dollar. "You're cool, man," he said. "What Kurt did, that was wrong. He can kind of go off sometimes, but I know where you're coming from. I like peace."

"I know you do," I said, "and I appreciate it."

It was the first time anyone had given me an entire dollar, and it occurred to me that if I could get beaten up twenty times a day, I could make some real money. Then I saw my broken glasses, and the equation fell apart. I was picking them off the ground when Dan stepped up, pretending to have missed the whole thing. "What happened to you?" he asked.

"Don't give me that," I said.

"Don't give you what?" He bit his lip to keep from laughing, and I knew in that moment that our friendship was over.

"Just call your mom," I said. "I'm ready to get out of here."

There were a million ways to hurt yourself at the state fair, so when my mother asked about my lip I told her I'd hit the safety bar while riding the Tilt-A-Whirl.

"Aren't you a little too old for that?" she

asked. She had the Tilt-A-Whirl confused with the twirling cups and saucers designed for grade-school kids. My mother had actually pictured me wedged into a flying teacup.

"Jesus," I said. "What do you take me for?"

She offered to have my glasses fixed but drew the line when I asked for a brand-new pair.

"But the ones I've got make me look like a bozo."

"Well, of course they do," she said. "They're glasses. That's their job."

Dan and I had planned to return to the fair on Sunday morning, but when he came to the door I sent him away, saying I wasn't feeling well. "I think I have some kind of flu."

"Could be the chicken pox," he said, and again he tried not to laugh. This was what you did to people you felt sorry for, to people too stupid to get the joke, and it was a lot worse than just coming out with it. He headed up the driveway and I thought again of the previous evening and of what I'd said after Kurt had thrown his first punch. Agreeing that I wasn't worth the energy it took to hit me was bad enough, but did I have to offer it as a matter of public record? *You can ask anybody.* It was no wonder he'd reared back and hit me again.

Late that night Dan knocked on my bedroom window. "Guess who made forty-four dollars?" he said. The bills were held behind his back, arranged into a droopy fan, and he brought them forth with great ceremony.

"Oh, come on. You did not make forty-four dollars." I denied it for the sake of argument, knowing that of course he had made forty-four dollars. The following weekend, his hair just that much longer, he would return to the fair and make even more. In no time he'd be wearing ponchos and sitting cross-legged before elaborate brass hookahs, our friendship as vague and insignificant to him as an old locker combination. "The two of you grew apart," my mother would say. She made it sound as if we'd veered off in different directions, though in fact we had the exact same destination. I just never made it.

It turned out that the vest was not suede but something closer to velveteen. This was a disappointment, but having suffered in its name, I had no choice but to buy it. With the money I had left over I got a pair

109

of blue corduroy hip-huggers, which made an ironic statement when worn with the red vest and a white shirt. *I love America. Yeah, right!*

"Tell me you're not wearing that out of the house," my mother said. I thought she was in some way jealous. Her youth gone, style was beyond her grasp, and she hated to see me enjoying the things that she could not.

"Could you please stop hassling me," I said.

"Ooh, *hassled*, are we?" She sighed and poured herself a glass of wine from the gallon jug in the pantry. "Go on then, Uncle Sam," she said. "Don't let me stop you."

I debuted my new outfit at the Kwik Pik, where once again I ran into the hippie girl. She wasn't begging this time, just standing with a friend and smoking cigarettes. Hanging out. I nodded hello, and as I passed she called me a teenybopper, meaning, in effect, that I was a poseur. The two of them cracked up laughing, and I burned with the particular shame that comes with being fourteen years old and realizing that your mother was right.

The last thing I wanted was to pass the hippie again, and so I stayed in the Kwik

Pik as long as I could, biding my time until the manager kicked me out. How was it that one moment you could look so good and the next you would give almost anything to crawl into your grocer's freezer, settling beneath the pot pies until you reached that mysterious age at which a person could truly think for himself. It would be so peaceful, more drowsing than actual sleeping. Every so often you'd come to and notice that the styles had changed. The shag had arrived. Beards were out. You would look at the world as if through the window of a bus, hopping out at that moment of time you instinctively recognized as your own. Here was the point where, without even trying, you could just be yourself and admit that you liked country music or hated the thought of hair against your neck. You could look and act however you wanted, and spend all day in the Kwik Pik if you felt like it. On leaving, you'd pass a woman dressed in a floor-length skirt, the paisley pattern resembling germs as seen through a microscope. A beaded headband, delicate wire-rimmed glasses: she'd ask you for a quarter, and you'd laugh, not cruelly, but politely, softly, as if she were telling a joke you had already heard.

Hejira

It wasn't anything I had planned on, but at the age of twenty-two, after dropping out of my second college and traveling across the country a few times, I found myself back in Raleigh, living in my parents' basement. After six months spent waking at noon, getting high, and listening to the same Joni Mitchell record over and over again, I was called by my father into his den and told to get out. He was sitting very formally in a big, comfortable chair behind his desk, and I felt as though he were firing me from the job of being his son.

I'd been expecting this to happen, and it honestly didn't bother me all that much. The way I saw it, being kicked out of the house was just what I needed if I was ever going to get back on my feet. "Fine," I said, "I'll go. But one day you'll be sorry."

I had no idea what I meant by this. It just seemed like the sort of thing a person should say when he was being told to leave.

My sister Lisa had an apartment over by the university and said that I could come stay with her as long as I didn't bring my Joni Mitchell record. My mother offered to drive me over, and after a few bong hits I took her up on it. It was a fifteen-minute trip across town, and on the way we listened to the rebroadcast of a radio call-in show in which people phoned the host to describe the various birds gathered around their backyard feeders. Normally the show came on in the morning, and it seemed strange to listen to it at night. The birds in question had gone to bed hours ago and probably had no idea they were still being talked about. I chewed this over and wondered if anyone back at the house was talking about *me*. To the best of my knowledge, no one had ever tried to imitate my voice or describe the shape of my head, and it was depressing that I went unnoticed while a great many people seemed willing to drop everything for a cardinal.

My mother pulled up in front of my sister's apartment building, and when I opened the car door she started to cry, which worried me, as she normally didn't do things like that. It wasn't one of those "I'm going to miss you" things, but something sadder and more desperate than that.

I wouldn't know it until months later, but my father had kicked me out of the house not because I was a bum but because I was gay. Our little talk was supposed to be one of those defining moments that shape a person's adult life, but he'd been so uncomfortable with the most important word that he'd left it out completely, saying only, "I think we both know why I'm doing this." I guess I could have pinned him down, I just hadn't seen the point. "Is it because I'm a failure? A drug addict? A sponge? Come on, Dad, just give me one good reason."

Who wants to say that?

My mother assumed that I knew the truth, and it tore her apart. Here was yet another defining moment, and again I missed it entirely. She cried until it sounded as if she were choking. "I'm sorry," she said. "I'm sorry, I'm sorry, I'm sorry."

I figured that within a few weeks I'd have a job and some crummy little apartment. It didn't seem insurmountable, but my mother's tears made me worry that finding these things might be a little harder than I thought. Did she honestly think I was that much of a loser?

"Really," I said, "I'll be fine."

The car light was on and I wondered what the passing drivers thought as they watched my mother sob. What kind of people did they think we were? Did they think she was one of those crybaby moms who fell apart every time someone chipped a coffee cup? Did they assume I'd said something to hurt her? Did they see us as just another crying mother and her stoned gay son, sitting in a station wagon and listening to a call-in show about birds, or did they imagine, for just one moment, that we might be special?

Slumus Lordicus

When she felt certain that she had seen every black-and-white movie ever made, my mother signed up for cable and began watching late-night infomercials in the kitchen. My father would wander up from the basement at about four, and the two of them would spend a pleasant half hour making fun of whatever happened to be on. "Give me a break," they'd chuckle. "Please!"

The only such program they managed to take seriously was hosted by a self-made man who had earned a fortune in real estate and addressed his studio audience as if they were students cramming for a final. The blackboard was in constant use. Charts and graphs were pointed at with a stick, but no matter how many times he explained it, I simply could not understand what the guy was talking about. It seemed that by refinancing his house, he had bought seventeen more, which were then rented out, allowing him to snatch up a shopping center and several putt-putt courses. If you went through his pockets, you'd be lucky to find twenty dollars, but on paper he was worth millions. Or so he claimed.

If accumulating property were truly this easy, it seemed that everyone would be following the millionaire's advice, but that was the catch: not everyone was awake at four a.m. While the rest of the world was fast sleep, you, the viewer, had chosen to better yourself, and wasn't that half the battle? I was between apartments at the time and saw the program twice before I left my parents' house and moved into a place of my own. That was the spring of 1980. A year later my mother and father owned a dozen duplexes on the south side of Raleigh, and were on their way.

We called our parents slumlords, but in fact the duplexes were not bad-looking. Each unit featured a bay window, parquet floors, and a fair-size yard shaded with trees. When first built, they were occupied by white people, but the neighborhood had changed since then, and with the exception of an elderly shut-in, all of the tenants were black. A few had jobs, but most were on public assistance, which meant, for us, that their rent was paid by the government, and usually on time.

The idea had been for my parents to work as a team — she would handle the leases, and he would see to any repairs. I assumed that, like always, my father would take over and do everything himself, but for once he acted according to plan. Deeds were signed, and within a month my mother was fluent in the various acronyms of the state and federal housing departments. Forms arrived, and the duplicates were sorted into stacks, the overflow spilling from the basement den to my former bedroom, which now served as a makeshift office. "Should this go under RHA or FHA?" my mother would ask. "Does B.J. qualify for AFDC or just the SSI?" She'd sit at the desk, her elbows smudged with copier fluid, and I'd feel sorry for everyone involved.

On a selfish note, "The Empire," as we liked to call it, provided me with an occasional job — a week of painting or weatherproofing or digging up a yard in search of a pipe. The downside was that I'd be doing these things for my father, meaning that the pay was negotiable. I'd present a time card, and he would dispute it, whittling my hours to a figure he considered more reasonable. "You expect me to believe you were there every day from nine until five? No lunch, no cigarette breaks, no sitting in the closet with your finger up your nose?"

The video monitor in my head would show me engaging in these very activities, and he would somehow catch a glimpse of it. "I knew it. I'll pay you for thirty hours, and that's just because I'm nice."

If we'd agreed on a flat rate — say, $300 in cash to paint an apartment — I might wind up with a check for $220, to be followed at the end of the year by a 1099-MISC form. Every job ended in an argument, my empty threats and petty name-calling put on ice and saved for the ride home. The tenants would have loved to watch us screaming at each other, and so we did our best to deny them that pleasure. Alone in the car we were savages, but at The Empire we were ambassadors for our race, acting not like the normal white people we'd grown up with but like the exceptional white people we vaguely remembered from random episodes of *Masterpiece Theatre*. Doors were held open, and great blocks of time were spent encouraging each other to go first.

"After you, Father."

"On the contrary, son, after *you*."

Were it not for my mother, we might have stood there all day. "Just go into the damned apartment!" she'd shout. "Jesus Christ, you two are like a couple of old ladies."

When it came to The Empire, my parents' roles were oddly reversed. My mother was still the more personable one, but if a tenant wanted any kind of a break, he soon learned to go to my father, who displayed a level of compassion we rarely saw at home. His own children couldn't get a dime out of him, but if Chester Kingsley lost his wallet or Regina Potts broke her collarbone, he was more than willing to work something out. When Dora Ward fell behind on her rent, he gave her an extension, then another, and another. On discovering she had moved out in the middle of the night, taking the stove and refrigerator with her, he said only, "Oh, well. They needed to be replaced anyway."

"The hell they did," my mother said. "That stove was only two years old. What kind of a landlord are you?"

I'd hoped to make money remodeling Dora's empty apartment, but the dream died when an interracial couple showed up, introducing themselves as Lance and Belinda Taylor. My parents and I were as-

120

sessing the empty kitchen when they knocked on the door, asking for a tour and announcing in the same breath that they loved the place just the way it was. All it needed was a stove and refrigerator, and everything else they could take care of on their own. "Carpentry and whatnot, that's what I do," Lance said. He offered his hands as proof, and we noted that the palms were thickly callused.

"Now show them the other side," his wife said. "Let them see your knuckles and whatever."

My mother suggested that the couple come back in a few months, but my father saw something almost biblical in their situation. A carpenter and his wife in search of shelter: all they lacked was an exhausted donkey. He moaned when told they were living in a motel, and buckled completely when shown a photo of the couple's three children. "We were going to touch the place up a little, but what can I say? You've got me."

"Let's just think about this," my mother said, but my father had thought enough. Lance paid the deposit in cash, and he and his family moved in the following day.

On seeing his new neighbors, Chester confided that it was the kids he felt sorry for. "Them and the husband. I mean, is that white woman ugly, or what?"

My father took the high road and tried to talk him out of it. "Oh, you don't mean that."

"Yes, he does," my mother said.

They did make for an odd-looking couple, not because of their color but because they were physically so mismatched. Lance was handsome and accustomed to being admired, while Belinda was gaunt and, "well," my mother said, "*unfortunate* looking. That's the kindest way to describe her, isn't it."

When they first moved in, the Taylors were polite and gung ho. Could they plant a vegetable garden? Certainly! Paint the living room? Why not? But the garden was never sown, and the paint cans sat untouched. They fought often, and loudly, and more than once the police arrived to pull the couple apart. The first time he fell behind in his rent, Lance called the house, demanding that my father distribute pebbles over his driveway. "I'm not paying three hundred dollars a month to walk over crushed oyster shells," he said. "It's bad for my tires *and* for my shoes, and before you get any more of my money, I want something done."

Distributing pebbles over Lance's drive-way meant distributing pebbles over everyone's driveway, and it surprised us all when my father agreed.

"I'm not talking cheap pebbles, either," Lance said. "I want the nice kind."

"You mean gravel," my father said.

"Yeah. That."

The driveway was hardly urgent, but still it was heartening to hear someone stick up for himself. This was exactly the sort of thing my father would have done had he been the tenant, and in admitting it, he was forced into a grudging admiration. "The guy's got gumption," he said. "There's no doubt about it."

A dump truck was sent, and I spent three days slowly spreading gravel. Lance paid his rent and called a few months later, complaining that birds were congregating in the tree outside his bedroom window. Had they been vultures, we may have seen his point, but these were songbirds, whose only crime was happiness.

"What do you want me to do?" my father asked. "Come down there in person and scare them away? Birds are a part of life, buddy. You've just got to learn to get along with them."

Lance insisted that the tree be cut down,

and when told no, he went ahead and did it himself. It was just a pine, not necessarily old or beautiful, but that didn't matter to my father, who loves trees and admires them the way playboys admire women. "Will you look at that!" he'll say, pulling to a stop at a busy intersection.

"Look at what?"

"What do you mean, 'Look at what?' The maple, idiot. She's a knockout."

When told what Lance had done, my father retreated to his bedroom, staring at the oaks outside the window. "Trimming is one thing," he said. "But to cut something down? To actually *end* its life? What kind of an animal *is* this guy?"

Lance felled the tree with a hatchet and left it where it lay. A few weeks later, now a month behind on his rent, he complained that rats were nesting in the branches. "I'll call the city and report you," he said to my father. "And if one of my kids gets bitten, I'll call the city *and* my lawyers."

"His lawyers, right!" my father said.

My mother had tried to look on the bright side, but now she worried that Lance might bite the children himself. In talking to other landlords, she'd come to identify him as a type, the sort of tenant who'd live rent-free, biding his time until he eventually bled you dry. If there was a skill to renting out property, it was the ability to spot such a person and never let him through the front door. Lance and his wife had made it in, and now my parents would have to get rid of them, delicately and by the book. They didn't want to give the Taylors any ammunition, and so it was agreed that the tree would be removed. "I really don't see any other way," my mother said. "The son of a bitch says jump, and we'll just have to do it."

I went with my father to cut it up and carry it away, and from the moment we arrived I had the distinct feeling that we were being watched. It was like one of those scenes from a Western — high noon and the street was empty. "Be cool," my father said, more to himself than to me. "We'll just do our job and be on our way."

We'd been at it for all of ten minutes when Lance stepped out, dressed in jeans and toffee-colored cowboy boots. Maybe the boots were too small or not yet broken in, but for whatever reason he moved slowly and tentatively, as if walking were new to him.

"Here we go," my father said.

Lance's first complaint was that the

noise of the chain saw was disturbing his children, one of whom was supposedly sick with the flu.

"In *September?*" my father asked.

"My kids can get sick any damn time they want," Lance said. "I'm just warning you to keep it down." There was no way to keep down a chain saw, but that wasn't really the point. My father had been put on notice within earshot of the other tenants, and now there would be complications.

Lance hobbled back into his apartment and reappeared a short while later. The boots were gone now, and in their place he wore a pair of sneakers. I was dragging a branch toward the curb, and he complained that in doing so, I was disturbing the integrity of his yard, which was alternately bald and overgrown and had all the integrity of a litter box. "You need to *lift* those branches," he said. "One of them touches the ground and you'll be answering to me. Understand?"

My father was a good six inches shorter than Lance, and he raised his head skyward in order to meet the man's eyes. "Hey," he said. "Don't you talk to my son that way."

"Well, you talked to *my* son that way," Lance said. "You called him a liar. Said there was no way he could have the flu in September."

"Well, I didn't say it to *him*," my father said.

"It's the same thing. You talk shit to my son and I'll talk shit to yours."

"Oh, come on," my father said. "There's no need for that kind of language."

They started talking at the same time, and when my father raised his voice Lance accused him of shouting. "You can't yell at me," he said. "Plantation days are over. I'm not your slave." This was played to the balcony, his arms cast toward the neighboring windows.

"Who are you *talking* to?" my father asked.

"You think I'm just some nigger you can shout at? Is that what you're saying, that I'm a nigger? Are you calling me a nigger?"

I had never heard my father use this word, so it was doubly unfair for Lance to put it into his mouth. People would talk, and in time it would seem that my father *had* called Lance a nigger. This is the nature of storytelling, and nothing can be done about it.

"You're out of your mind," my father said.

"Oh, so now I'm a crazy nigger. Is that it?"

"I didn't say that."

"No, but you're *thinking* it."

My father abandoned his good manners. "You're full of crap," he said.

"Oh, so I'm a liar?"

They were inches apart now, the toes of their shoes almost touching. In the distance, I could see Belinda standing at her window, and Chester standing at his. Regina Potts, Donald Pullman: all of them had the same eager expression. Were someone threatening my landlord, I'd have been thrilled, too, but this was my father we were talking about, and so I hated them for looking so thoroughly entertained.

I don't remember what prompted my father and Lance to cool down, but it happened, gradually, like a kettle taken off the burner. Balled fists slackened to hands, the distance between them grew wider, and little by little their voices lowered to a normal register. My immediate sensation was relief. I didn't have to do anything. I had been spared the indignity, the responsibility, of watching my father engage in a fight. The thought of him throwing a punch was bad enough, but the thought of him losing — my father pressed to the ground, my father calling out in pain or surprise — was unbearable.

My new worry was that this was not over. We'd gotten through today, but what would happen the next time Lance and my father ran into each other? A person who wore cowboy boots and cut down trees in order to displace birds was likely capable of anything: a surprise attack, loosened lug nuts, a firebomb. They were reasonable fears, but if any of them occurred to my father, he did not show it. When Lance walked away, he simply put on his gloves and went back to work, as if this had been just any ordinary interruption — Chester wanting him to check a leaky faucet, the Barrett sisters asking if we could come and clean out their gutters. It may have been different for Lance, but my father didn't live like this. There were no shoving matches at IBM or the Raleigh Country Club, and while he was aggressive in smaller ways — ramming people's carts at the grocery store, yelling at other drivers to get a Seeing Eye dog — I think it had been a long time since he had seriously considered a fight. All he said was "Can you beat that?" and then he shook his head and revved up the chain saw.

The sun was setting as we piled the logs into the bed of the truck. My father fished the keys from his pocket, and we sat in the cab for a few minutes before heading home. Over at Minnie Edwards's, a child opened the door to a live-in boyfriend who was not supposed to be there. This sort of thing was of interest to the welfare department, especially when the boyfriend held a job and contributed to the running of the household. Every so often, a caseworker would come around, looking for men's clothing or evidence of wild spending, and it was assumed that my family shared this interest. The man entered Minnie's apartment, and a moment later she stepped outside and gestured to my father to roll down his window. "He's my brother," she said. "Home from the army." All this hiding. All this exhausting explanation.

"So what do you think?" my father said. He wasn't talking about Lance or Minnie Edwards's boyfriend, but all of it. Everything before us was technically ours — the lawns, the houses, the graveled driveways. This was what ingenuity had bought: a corner of the world that could, in time, expand, growing lot by lot until you could drive for some distance and never lose your feelings of guilt and uncertainty.

Lance and his family would eventually leave the apartment, but not before what had seemed to be a perfectly fine bathroom ceiling fell with no provocation upon his wife's head. She would limp into court, ridiculous and so predictable with her bandages and neck brace, but the jury would fall for it and award her a settlement. We'd later hear that the two of them had broken up. That he had taken off with someone else. That she was changing beds in a hotel. Chester, too, would eventually break up with his wife and leave with not just the appliances but the storm windows as well.

Troubles moved on only to be replaced by new ones, and looking out the windshield, my father seemed to see them all: the woman whose son would set fire to his bedroom, the man who'd throw a car battery through his neighbor's window, a frenetic blur of hostile tenants, dismantling his empire brick by brick.

"I was going to help you out if Lance, you know, hit you or anything," I said.

"Of course you were," my father said, and for a moment he even allowed himself to believe it. "The guy didn't know what he was up against, did he?"

"No, he didn't."

"The two of us together, man oh man, what a sight that would have been!" We laughed then, Vespasian and Titus in the cab of a Toyota pickup. My father patted my knee and then pulled the truck away from the curb. "I'll give you a check when we get home," he said. "But don't think I'm going to pay you for standing there with your mouth open. It doesn't work that way. Not with me it doesn't."

The Girl Next Door

"Well, that little experiment is over," my mother said. "You tried it, it didn't work out, so what do you say we just move on." She was dressed in her roll-up-the-shirtsleeves outfit: the faded turquoise skirt, a cotton head scarf, and one of the sporty blouses my father had bought in the hope she might take up golf. "We'll start with the kitchen," she said. "That's always the best way, isn't it."

I was moving again. This time because of the neighbors.

"Oh, no," my mother said. "They're not to blame. Let's be honest now." She liked to take my problems back to the source, which was usually me. Like, for instance, when I got food poisoning it wasn't the chef's fault. "*You're* the one who wanted to go Oriental. *You're* the one who ordered the lomain."

"Lo mein. It's two words."

"Oh, he speaks Chinese now! Tell me, Charlie Chan, what's the word for six straight hours of vomiting and diarrhea?"

What she meant was that I'd tried to save money. The cheap Chinese restaurant, the seventy-five-dollar-a-month apartment: "Cut corners and it'll always come back to bite you in the ass." That was one of her sayings. But if you didn't *have* money how could you *not* cut corners?

"And whose fault is it that you don't have any money? I'm not the one who turned up his nose at a full-time job. I'm not the one who spends his entire paycheck down at the hobby shop."

"I understand that."

"Well, good," she said, and then we began to wrap the breakables.

In my version of the story, the problem began with the child next door, a third-grader who, according to my mother, was bad news right from the start. "Put it together," she'd said when I first called to tell her about it. "Take a step back. Think."

But what was there to think about? She was a nine-year-old girl.

"Oh, they're the worst," my mother said. "What's her name? Brandi? Well, that's cheap, isn't it."

"I'm sorry," I said, "but aren't I talking to someone who named her daughter *Tiffany?*"

"My hands were tied!" she shouted. "The damned Greeks had me against the wall and you know it."

"Whatever you say."

"So this girl," my mother continued — and I knew what she would ask before she even said it. "What does her father do?"

I told her there wasn't a father, at least not one that I knew about, and then I waited as she lit a fresh cigarette. "Let's see," she said. "Nine-year-old girl named after an alcoholic beverage. Single mother in a neighborhood the police won't even go to. What else have you got for me?" She spoke as if I'd formed these people out of clay, as if it were my fault that the girl was nine years old and her mother couldn't keep a husband. "I don't suppose this woman has a job, does she?"

"She's a bartender."

"Oh, that's splendid," my mother said. "Go on."

The woman worked nights and left her daughter alone from four in the afternoon until two or three in the morning. Both were blond, their hair almost white, with invisible eyebrows and lashes. The mother darkened hers with pencil, but the girl appeared to have none at all. Her face was like the weather in one of those places with no discernible seasons. Every now and then, the circles beneath her eyes would shade to purple. She might show up with a fat lip or a scratch on her neck but her features betrayed nothing.

You had to feel sorry for a girl like that. No father, no eyebrows, and that mother. Our apartments shared a common wall, and every night I'd hear the woman stomping home from work. Most often she was with someone, but whether alone or with company she'd find some excuse to bully her daughter out of bed. Brandi had left a doughnut on the TV or Brandi had forgotten to drain her bathwater. They're important lessons to learn, but there's something to be said for leading by example. I never went into their apartment, but what I saw from the door was pretty rough — not simply messy or chaotic, but hopeless, the lair of a depressed person.

Given her home life, it wasn't surprising that Brandi latched onto me. A normal mother might have wondered what was up — her nine-year-old daughter spending time with a twenty-six-year-old man — but this one didn't seem to care. I was just free stuff to her: a free babysitter, a free cigarette machine, the whole store. I'd hear her through the wall sometimes: "Hey, go ask your friend for a roll of toilet paper." "Go ask your friend to make you a sandwich." If company was coming and she wanted to be alone, she'd kick the girl out. "Why don't you go next door and see what your little playmate is up to?"

Before I moved in, Brandi's mother had used the couple downstairs, but you could tell that the relationship had soured. Next to the grocery carts chained to their porch was a store-bought sign, the NO TRESPASSING followed by a handwritten "This meens you, Brandi!!!!"

There was a porch on the second floor as well, with one door leading to Brandi's bedroom and another door leading to mine. Technically, the two apartments were supposed to share it, but the entire thing was taken up with their junk, and so I rarely used it.

"I can't wait until you get out of your little slumming phase," my mother had said on first seeing the building. She spoke as if she'd been raised in splendor, but in fact her childhood home had been much worse. The suits she wore, the delicate bridges holding her teeth in place — it was all an invention. "You live in bad neighborhoods so you can feel superior," she'd say, the introduction, always, to a fight. "The point is to move *up* in the world. Even sideways will do in a pinch, but what's the point in moving down?"

As a relative newcomer to the middle class, she worried that her children might slip back into the world of public assistance and bad teeth. The finer things were not yet in our blood, or at least that was the way she saw it. My thrift-shop clothing drove her up the wall, as did the second-hand mattress lying without benefit of box springs upon my hardwood floor. "It's not *ironic*," she'd say. "It's not *ethnic*. It's filthy."

Bedroom suites were fine for people like my parents, but as an artist I preferred to rough it. Poverty lent my little dabblings a much-needed veneer of authenticity, and I imagined myself repaying the debt by gently lifting the lives of those around me, not en masse but one by one, the old-fashioned way. It was, I thought, the least I could do.

I told my mother that I had allowed Brandi into my apartment, and she sighed deeply into her end of the telephone. "And I bet you gave her the grand tour, didn't you? Mr. Show-Off. Mr. Big Shot." We had a huge fight over that one. I didn't call her for two days. Then the phone rang.

"Brother," she said. "You have no idea what you're getting yourself into."

A neglected girl comes to your door and what are you supposed to do, turn her away?

"Exactly," my mother said. "Throw her the hell out."

But I couldn't. What my mother defined as boasting, I considered a standard show-and-tell. "This is my stereo system," I'd said to Brandi. "This is the electric skillet I received last Christmas, and here's a little something I picked up in Greece last summer." I thought I was exposing her to the things a regular person might own and appreciate, but all she heard was the possessive. "This is my honorable-mention ribbon," meaning "It belongs to *me*. It's not yours." Every now and then I'd give her a little something, convinced that she'd treasure it forever. A postcard of the Acropolis, prestamped envelopes, packaged towelettes bearing the insignia of Olympic Airlines. "Really?" she'd say. "For me?"

The only thing she owned, the only thing special, was a foot-tall doll in a clear plastic carrying case. It was a dime-store version of one of those Dolls from Many Countries, this one Spanish with a beet red dress and a droopy mantilla on her head. Behind her, printed on cardboard, was the place where she lived: a piñata-lined street snaking up the hill to a dusty bullring. The doll had been given to her by her grandmother, who was forty years old and lived in a trailer beside an army base.

"What is this?" my mother asked. "A skit from *Hee Haw*? Who the hell *are* these people?"

"These people," I said, "are my neighbors, and I'd appreciate it if you wouldn't make fun of them. The grandmother doesn't need it, I don't need it, and I'm pretty sure a nine-year-old-girl doesn't need it, either." I didn't tell her that the grandmother was nicknamed Rascal or that, in the picture Brandi showed me, the woman was wearing cutoff shorts and an ankle bracelet.

"We don't talk to her anymore," Brandi had said when I handed back the picture. "She's out of our life, and we're glad of it." Her voice was dull and robotic, and I got the impression that the line had been fed to her by her mother. She used a similar tone when introducing her doll. "She's not for playing with. She's for display."

Whoever imposed this rule had obviously backed it up with a threat. Brandi would trace her finger along the outside of the box, tempting herself, but never once did I see her lift the lid. It was as if the doll would explode if removed from her natural environment. Her world was the box, and a strange world it was.

"See," Brandi said one day, "she's on her way home to cook up those clams."

She was talking about the castanets dangling from the doll's wrist. It was a funny thought, childish, and I probably should have let it go rather than playing the know-it-all. "If she were an American doll those might be clams," I said. "But instead she's from Spain, and those are called castanets." I wrote the word on a piece of paper. "Castanets, look it up."

"She's not from Spain, she's from Fort Bragg."

"Well, maybe she was *bought* there," I said. "But she's supposed to be Spanish."

"And what's *that* supposed to mean?" It was hard to tell without the eyebrows, but I think she was mad at me.

"It's not *supposed* to mean anything," I said. "It's just true."

"You're full of it. There's no such place."

"Sure there is," I said. "It's right next to France."

"Yeah, right. What's that, a store?"

I couldn't believe I was having this conversation. How could you not know that Spain was a country? Even if you were nine years old, it seems you would have picked it up on TV or something. "Oh, Brandi," I said. "We've got to find you a map."

Because I couldn't do it any other way, we fell into a tight routine. I had a part-time construction job and would return home at exactly 5:30. Five minutes later Brandi would knock on my door, and stand there blinking until I let her in. I was going through a little wood-carving phase at the time, whittling figures whose heads resembled the various tools I worked with during the day: a hammer, a hatchet, a wire brush. Before beginning, I'd arrange some paper and colored pencils on my desk. "Draw your doll," I'd say. "Copy the bullring in her little environment. Express yourself!" I encouraged Brandi to broaden her horizons, but she usually quit after the first few minutes, claiming it was too much work.

Mainly she observed, her eyes shifting between my knife and the Spanish doll parked before her on the desktop. She'd talk about how stupid her teachers were, and then she'd ask what I would do if I had a million dollars. If I'd had a million dollars at that time in my life I probably would have spent every last penny of it on drugs, but I didn't admit it, because I wanted to set a good example. "Let's see," I'd say. "If I had that kind of money, I'd probably give it away."

"Yeah, right. You'd what, just hand it out to people on the street?"

"No, I'd set up a foundation and try to make a difference in people's lives." At this one even the doll was gagging.

When asked what she'd do with a million dollars, Brandi described cars and gowns and heavy bracelets encrusted with gems.

"But what about others? Don't you want to make them happy?"

"No. I want to make them jealous."

"You don't mean that," I'd say.

"Try me."

"Oh, Brandi." I'd make her a glass of chocolate milk and she'd elaborate on her list until 6:55, when friendship period was officially over. If work had gone slowly and there weren't many shavings to sweep up, I might let her stay an extra two minutes, but never longer.

"Why do I have to go right this second?" she asked one evening. "Are you going to work or something?"

"Well, no, not exactly."

"Then what's your hurry?"

I never should have told her. The good part about being an obsessive compulsive is that you're always on time for work. The bad part is that you're on time for everything. Rinsing your coffee cup, taking a bath, walking your clothes to the Laundromat: there's no mystery to your comings and goings, no room for spontaneity. During that time of my life I went to the IHOP every evening, heading over on my bike at exactly seven and returning at exactly nine. I never ate there, just drank coffee, facing the exact same direction in the exact same booth and reading library books for exactly an hour. After this I would ride to the grocery store. Even if I didn't need anything I'd go, because that's what that time was allotted for. If the lines were short, I'd bike home the long way or circle the block a few times, unable to return early, as those five or ten minutes weren't scheduled for apartment time.

"What would happen if you were ten minutes late?" Brandi asked. My mother often asked the same question — everyone did. "You think the world will fall apart if you walk through that door at nine-o-four?"

144

They said it jokingly, but the answer was yes, that's exactly what I thought would happen. The world would fall apart. On the nights when another customer occupied my regular IHOP booth, I was shattered. "Is there a problem?" the waitress would ask, and I'd find that I couldn't even speak.

Brandi had been incorporated into my schedule for a little over a month when I started noticing that certain things were missing — things like pencil erasers and these little receipt books I'd picked up in Greece. In searching through my drawers and cabinets, I discovered that other things were missing as well: a box of tacks, a key ring in the form of a peanut.

"I see where this is going," my mother said. "The little sneak unlatched your porch door and wandered over while you were off at the pancake house. That's what happened, isn't it?"

I hated that she figured it out so quickly.

When I confronted Brandi, she broke down immediately. It was as if she'd been dying to confess, had rehearsed it, even. The stammered apology, the plea for mercy. She hugged me around the waist, and when she finally pulled away I felt my shirtfront, expecting to find it wet with tears. It wasn't. I don't know why I did what I did next, or rather, I guess I do. It was all part of my ridiculous plan to set a good example. "You know what we have to do now, don't you?" I sounded firm and fair until I considered the consequences, at which point I faltered. "We've got to go . . . and tell your mother what you just *did?*"

I half hoped that Brandi might talk me out of it, but instead she just shrugged.

"I bet she did," my mother said. "I mean, come on, you might as well have reported her to the cat. What did you expect that mother to do, needlepoint a sampler with the Ten Commandments? Wake up, Dopey, the woman's a whore."

Of course she was right. Brandi's mother listened with her arms crossed, a good sign until I realized that her anger was directed toward me rather than her daughter. In the far corner of the room a long-haired man cleaned beneath his fingernails with a pair of scissors. He looked my way for a moment and then turned his attention back to the television.

"So she took a pencil eraser," Brandi's mother said. "What do you want me to do, dial nine-one-one?" She made it sound unbelievably petty.

"I just thought you should know what happened," I said.

"Well, lucky me. Now I know."

I returned to my apartment and pressed my ear against the bedroom wall. "Who was that?" the guy asked.

"Oh, just some asshole," Brandi's mother said.

Things cooled down after that. I could forgive Brandi for breaking into my apartment, but I could not forgive her mother. *Just some asshole.* I wanted to go to the place where she worked and burn it down. In relating the story, I found myself employing lines I'd probably heard on public radio. "Children *want* boundaries," I said. "They *need* them." It sounded sketchy to me, but everyone seemed to agree — especially my mother, who suggested that in this particular case, a five-by-eleven cell might work. She wasn't yet placing the entire blame on me, so it was still enjoyable to tell her things, to warm myself in the comforting glow of her outrage.

The next time Brandi knocked I pretended to be out — a ploy that fooled no one. She called my name, figured out where this was headed, and then went home to watch TV. I didn't plan to stay mad forever. A few weeks of the silent treatment and then I figured we'd pick up where we left off. In the meantime, I occasionally passed her in the front yard, just standing there as if she were waiting for someone normal to pick her up. I'd say, "Hello, how's it going?" and she'd give me this tight little smile, the sort you'd offer if someone you hated was walking around with chocolate stains on the back of his pants.

Back when our neighborhood was prosperous, the building we lived in was a single-family home, and sometimes I liked to imagine it as it once was: with proud rooms and chandeliers, a stately working household serviced by maids and coachmen. I was carrying out the trash one afternoon and came upon what used to be the coal cellar, a grim crawl space now littered with shingles and mildewed cardboard boxes. There were worn-out fuses and balls of electrical wire, and there, in the back, a pile of objects I recognized as my own: things I hadn't noticed were missing — photographs, for instance, and slides of my bad artwork. Moisture had fouled the casings, and when I backed out of the cellar and held them to the sun I saw that the film had been scratched, not by accident but intentionally, with a pin or a razor. "Yur a asshole," one of them read. "Suk my dick why don't you." The spelling was all over the place, the writing tiny and furious, bleeding into the mind-bending designs spewed by mental patients who don't know when to stop. It was the exact effect I'd been striving for in my bland imitation folk art, so not only did I feel violated, I felt jealous. I mean, this girl was the real thing.

There were pages of slides, all of them etched with ugly messages. Photographs, too, were ruined. Here was me as a toddler with the word *shity* scratched into my forehead. Here was my newlywed mother netting crabs with her eyes clawed out. Included in the pile were all of the little presents accepted with such false gratitude, the envelopes and postcards, even the towelettes, everything systematically destroyed.

I gathered it all up and went straight to Brandi's mother. It was two o'clock in the afternoon and she was dressed in one of those thigh-length robes people wear when practicing karate. This was morning for her, and she stood drinking cola from a tall glass mug. "Fuck," she said. "Haven't we been through this?"

"Well, actually, no." My voice was higher than normal, and unstable. "Actually, we *haven't* been through this."

I'd considered myself an outsider in this neighborhood, something like a missionary among the savages, but standing there panting, my hair netted with cobwebs, I got the horrible feeling that I fit right in.

Brandi's mother glanced down at the filthy stack in my hand, frowning, as if these were things I was trying to sell door-to-door. "You know what?" she said. "I don't need this right now. No, you know what? I don't need it, period. Do you think having a baby was easy for me? I don't have nobody helping me out, a husband or day care or whatever, I'm all alone here, understand?"

I tried putting the conversation back on track, but as far as Brandi's mother was concerned, there was no other track. It was all about her. "I work my own hours *and* cover shifts for Kathy fucking Cornelius and on my one day off I've got some faggot hassling me about some shit I don't even *know* about? I don't think so. Not today I don't, so why don't you go find somebody else to dump on."

She slammed the door in my face and I stood in the hallway wondering, *Who is*

Kathy Cornelius? What just happened?

In the coming days I ran the conversation over and over in my mind, thinking of all the fierce and sensible things I should have said, things like "Hey, *I'm* not the one who decided to have children" and "It's not *my* problem that you have to cover shifts for Kathy fucking Cornelius."

"It wouldn't have made any difference," my mother said. "A woman like that, the way she sees it she's a victim. Everyone's against her, no matter what."

I was so angry and shaken that I left the apartment and went to stay with my parents on the other side of town. My mom drove me to the IHOP and back, right on schedule, but it wasn't the same. On my bike I was left to my own thoughts, but now I had her lecturing me, both coming and going. "What did you hope to gain by letting that girl into your apartment? And don't tell me you wanted to make a difference in her life, please, I just ate." I got it that night and then again the following morning. "Do you want me to give you a ride back to your little shantytown?" she asked, but I was mad at her, and so I took the bus.

I thought things couldn't get much worse, and then, that evening, they did. I was just returning from the IHOP and was on the landing outside Brandi's door when I heard her whisper, "Faggot." She had her mouth to the keyhole, and her voice was puny and melodic. It was the way I'd always imagined a moth might sound. "Faggot. What's the matter, faggot? What's wrong, huh?"

She laughed as I scrambled into my apartment, and then she ran to the porch and began to broadcast through my bedroom door. "Little faggot, little tattletale. You think you're so smart, but you don't know shit."

"That's it," my mother said. "We've got to get you out of there." There was no talk of going to the police or social services, just "Pack up your things. She won."

"But can't I . . ."

"Oh-ho no," my mother said. "You've got her mad now and there's no turning back. All she has to do is go to the authorities, saying you molested her. Is that what you want? One little phone call and your life is ruined."

"But I didn't do *anything*. I'm gay, remember?"

"That's not going to save you," she said. "Push comes to shove and who do you think they're going to believe, a nine-year-old girl or the full-grown man who gets his jollies carving little creatures out of balsa wood?"

"They're *not* little creatures!" I yelled. "They're tool people!"

"What the hell difference does it make? In the eyes of the law you're just some nut with a knife who sits in the pancake house staring at a goddam stopwatch. You dress that girl in something other than a tube top and prop her up on the witness stand — crying her eyes out — and what do you think is going to happen? Get that mother in on the act and you've got both a criminal trial *and* a civil suit on your hands."

"You watch too much TV."

"Not as much as they do," she said. "I can guaran-goddam-tee you that. You think these people can't smell money?"

"But I haven't got any."

"It's not your money they'll be after," she said. "It's mine."

"You mean Dad's." I was smarting over the "little creatures" comment and wanted to hurt her, but it didn't work.

"I mean *our* money," she said. "You think I don't know how these things work? I wasn't just born some middle-aged woman with a nice purse and a decent pair

153

of shoes. My God, the things you don't know. My *God*."

My new apartment was eight blocks away, facing our city's first Episcopal church. My mother paid the deposit and the first month's rent and came with her station wagon to help me pack and move my things. Carrying a box of my feather-weight balsa-wood sculptures out onto the landing, her hair gathered beneath a gingham scarf, I wondered how she appeared to Brandi, who was certainly watching through the keyhole. What did she represent to her? The word *mother* wouldn't do, as I don't really think she understood what it meant. A person who shepherds you along the way and helps you out when you're in trouble — what would she call that thing? A queen? A crutch? A teacher?

I heard a noise from behind the door, and then the little moth voice. "Bitch," Brandi whispered.

I fled back into the apartment, but my mother didn't even pause. "Sister," she said, "you don't know the half of it."

Blood Work

For many years I cleaned apartments in New York, which is not a bad way to make a living. My boss ran a small agency and charged clients fifteen dollars an hour, five of which went to him and ten to the employee. You could earn more working for yourself, but to me it was worth it to have a middleman, someone to set up the schedule and take the occasional flak. If something got broken, our boss would replace it, and if something was stolen, or alleged to have been stolen, it was he who defended our character. With the exception of a chiropractor's office, all of my jobs were residential, apartments and lofts I visited once a week or once every other week. The owners were usually off at work, and on the few occasions that they were home they tried to make themselves as unobtrusive as possible, acting as though it were my apartment and they were just guests.

One such client was a claims adjuster in his mid-sixties. I'd been cleaning his apartment for over a year and finally met him while he was at home recovering from an operation. He had some kind of a heart condition and approached me while I was cleaning out his refrigerator. "I hate to bother you," he said, "but I'm going to go lie down for a while. I've set the alarm, but if for some reason I don't wake up, I'm wondering if you could possibly insert this into my anus." He handed me a rubber glove and a translucent lozenge filled with amber liquid.

"If you're not awake by when?" I asked.

"Oh, say, three o'clock."

He went into the bedroom and I started wondering what I'd do if the alarm failed to rouse him. Which was worse — inserting a lozenge into a stranger's anus or feeling responsible when his heart stopped beating? As with most things, I supposed it all depended upon the person. The man had never complained to my boss or asked me to do his laundry, and he *had* been thoughtful enough to provide me with a rubber glove, so who was I to deny him this one favor?

The alarm sounded at three, and just as I was screwing up my courage, the claims adjuster stepped out of the bedroom, looking refreshed and ready to take on the afternoon. The following week he returned to work, and though I cleaned his apartment for another two years, we never saw each other again.

My boss was horrified by the suppository incident, but in retrospect I saw it as an adventure. It got sort of boring being alone all day, and so I asked to be sent on more jobs where the client was at home. Often these were one-shot deals. The apartment owner had hosted a particularly rowdy party or recently had some plaster sanded and wanted someone to straighten up the mess. Once I went to the home of a former Playmate who needed help reorganizing her closets. We got to talking, and she showed me pictures of her three ex-husbands, explaining that her family motto was "Eat, drink, and remarry."

"That's old," my boss said, but I had never heard it before.

In December of 1992 a story I'd written was broadcast on NPR, and six months later the *New York Times* ran a little article headlined HE DOES RADIO *AND* WINDOWS. It came out on a Sunday morning, and by ten a.m. people began calling me at home, asking if I could come clean their apartments. Many of them had an ulterior motive and wanted me to report on something they considered important or unfair: a discriminatory hiring practice, secret meetings held by their co-op board, a controversial medical breakthrough the bigwigs had chosen to suppress. "That's not really the kind of thing I do," I would tell them, but they were persistent and plied me with what they called "important contact numbers." This was always said in a whisper, implying that spies were everywhere.

When people phoned me at home I asked them to call my boss and set up an appointment through him. This proved my loyalty and weeded out some of the more obvious conspiracy theorists, who complained they were getting the runaround. A month after the article appeared, my boss left on vacation, and shortly afterward a stranger called, asking if I could possibly fit him in over the weekend. He gave me his name, Martin, and an address in the East Eighties. I offered to come at two o'clock on Sunday and after we'd hung up he called me again. "Is that two a.m. or two p.m.?" he asked.

"P.M.," I said. "Two in the afternoon."

I would later recognize this as the first sign of trouble.

The Upper East Side is dead on summer

weekends, and walking north from the subway station, I passed no more than a dozen people. Martin lived on the fifteenth floor of a newly built tower. A security guard announced my arrival, and as I stepped off the elevator, a man opened his door and stuck his head into the hall. He looked to be in his mid-forties, plump, with a round, sunburned face and damp, wheat-colored hair that was fine, like a baby's. Sweat soaked the underarms of his T-shirt, which fit him snugly around the stomach and pictured a sailboat in rough, tightly stretched waters. "Are you the one I talked to on the phone?" he asked.

I said that I was, and looking slightly disappointed, as if people like me were somehow the story of his life, he patted me on the back and introduced himself.

I thought that Martin had just returned from some sort of exercise, but walking into the apartment, I understood that his sweat was home-brewed. Outside it was in the high eighties, but his living room was at least ten degrees hotter. "It's like a pizza oven," he said. This was not offered as an apology. If anything, he sounded boastful. I looked at the air conditioner lying unplugged in the middle of the floor, at the row of closed windows offering a view of the neighboring high-rise.

"If you're hot, you can always . . ." He stuck his hands in the pockets of his shorts and looked down at his bare feet. "You can always . . . you know."

I guessed he meant that I could leave, but that seemed silly, seeing as I was already there. "That's all right," I told him. "I don't have air-conditioning, either."

"Oh, I *have* it," he said. "I just don't use it."

"Right."

"It came with the building," he said.

"That's nice."

"Nice if you like air-conditioning."

"Which you don't," I said.

"No," he said. "Not at all."

Normally, after a minute or two of small talk, the client would direct me toward the vacuum cleaner and make himself scarce. Martin continued to stare at his feet, and it occurred to me that if I were ever going to get out of there, I needed to take the lead. "If it's okay with you, I normally start with the kitchen," I said.

"Whatever you want." He walked toward the adjacent room and leaned against the doorjamb as I entered. You could tell immediately that the guy didn't cook. The stove looked brand-new, and aside from a Mr. Coffee machine, the countertop was bare.

"I'm normally not here on the weekends," he confided. "Not in the summer anyway."

I searched beneath the sink for cleaning supplies. "Oh, yeah?"

"Friday comes and I'm on the first bus to Fire Island," he said. "You ever go there? To FIRE ISLAND?"

He said *Fire Island* as if it were a prearranged code, the watchwords signaling me to hand over the microfilm. I told him I'd never been, and he took a seat on the countertop. "How can you not have gone to FIRE ISLAND?" he asked. "I thought *everybody* went there."

"Everybody but me." I opened his refrigerator, which was empty except for a jug of Diet Coke and dozens of doll-size bottles filled with clear serum. If forced to guess, I'd have said they were for some sort of a mental disorder. He simply would not let go of the Fire Island business.

"I can give you some information if you like," he said, and before I could decline he reached into a drawer and handed me a brochure. The cover pictured a dozen muscular men frolicking aboard the deck

161

of a pleasure craft. Each was shirtless, and several wore nothing but thongs. I understood that he wanted me to comment on them, but instead I pointed to a tiny figure, barely visible on the distant shore. "Is that a fisherman?" I asked.

"Well, it might be," Martin said. "But that's not really what FIRE ISLAND is about."

I handed the brochure back to him. "I'm too impatient to fish. Crabbing, though, I don't mind that. So, tell me, do you have any brothers and sisters?"

The change in topic seemed to throw him. "A sister. She lives in New Jersey. But on FIRE ISLAND, see, they have —"

"And what about your parents?"

"My father died a few years ago," he said. "But my mother's still around."

He didn't seem very eager to talk about it, and so I dug in, hoping he might go into the other room and leave me alone. "So who does your mother love more, you or your sister?"

"I don't know," he said. "What difference does it make?"

"Just curious. Do you ever take her out to Fire Island?"

"No."

"Well, okay then," I said.

Martin stuck the brochure back into the drawer and retreated to the living room, where he turned on the TV and flipped back and forth between channels. With him out of the way, I finished the kitchen in no time. Next came the bathroom and then the bedroom, which was airless and cluttered and felt even hotter than the rest of the apartment. The dresser was heaped with clothing and gay pornography, the alternating layers of shirts and magazines reminding me of science projects illustrating the earth's crust. I counted five blankets on the unmade bed and was trying to make sense of them when Martin walked in and took a seat on a folding chair. The conversation in the kitchen was behind him now, and he appeared eager to make a fresh start. "Look at you, so hard at work!"

"How can you sleep with five blankets?" I asked.

"Well," he said. "I have diabetes. I get cold."

I had never heard of this. "Do all diabetics feel cold in the summer?"

"You'll have to ask them." He reached into an open drawer and pulled out a plastic device the size of a Walkman. "I've got an idea," he said. "What do you say we test your blood sugar?"

"Now?"

"Sure," he said. "Why not?"

I could think of dozens of reasons.

"I just prick your finger, wipe the blood onto a bit of paper, and feed it into the machine. Come on, what do you say?"

"That's all right."

"But the needle is prepackaged," he said. "Completely sterile. You're not going to catch anything."

"Thanks for asking, but I think I'll pass."

I was trying to make the bed, and as I reached for a pillow he grabbed my wrist and stabbed me with his short needle. "Gotcha!" he said. Blood pooled on the tip of my index finger, and he swooped in to blot it with a small slip of paper. "Now we just feed it into the machine . . . and we wait."

The good news was that my blood sugar was normal. "You should count yourself lucky," Martin said. "Mine is all over the place." He showed me a scar on the crown of his head and told me of the time, several months earlier, when he'd awoken on the living-room floor, lying in a pool of blood. "Complete blackout," he said. "I must have hit the glass coffee table on my way down." A year before that, he'd passed out in the street and spent the night in the gutter. "With a condition like mine, anything can happen," he told me.

The implication was that he could not be held responsible for his actions. It was not a comforting message, but still I stayed, not because I felt sorry for him but because I didn't know how to leave. It would have been awkward — or rather, *more* awkward — and while I definitely thought about it, the mechanics were beyond me. Then, too, I couldn't help believe that I'd *deserved* to have my blood tested. I had asked whom his mother loved more, him or his sister. I'd thought I was clever, had prided myself on my ability to drive someone away, and this had been my punishment. The way I saw it, we were even.

When I'd finished with the bedroom, we moved on to the living room, Martin toddling two steps behind me. I gathered some scattered newspapers and magazines into a single pile and had just started dusting the TV when he sank down onto the sofa and activated a porno tape preset in the VCR. It was a military story. A buck private had failed to properly shine his sergeant's boots, and now there would be hell to pay. "You ever seen this?" Martin asked.

I told him I didn't have a VCR, and as he pulled off his shorts, I turned away.

My housecleaning role model was a woman named Lena Payne, who worked for my family in the late 1960s. I used to come home from school and watch with great interest as she tackled the kitchen floor. "Use a mop," my mother would say, "that's what I do," and Lena would lower her head in pity. She knew what my mother did not: either you want a clean floor or you want to use a mop, but you can't have both. Whether it was ironing or deciding how to punish a child, Lena knew best, and so she became indispensable. Like her, I wanted to control households and make people feel lazy and spoiled without ever coming out and saying so. "Didn't you have potato chips *yesterday?*" she'd ask, frowning at the can as big as a kettledrum my sisters and I parked in front of the TV. Suggesting that potato chips were an overindulged luxury caused them to lose their taste and meant there'd be fewer crumbs to vacuum at the end of the day. She was smart, and very good at her job. I worshipped her.

Standing in Martin's living room, the sweat dripping off my face, I wondered how Lena might have reacted had one of us peeled off our pants and proceeded to masturbate to a movie called *Fort Dicks*. We didn't have video back then, but if we did, I imagine she'd have said exactly what I had, "I don't have a VCR." It would have stopped *me*, but this guy was obviously wired differently.

Whack, whack, whack. Whack, whack, whack. Martin's forearm batted against a newspaper lying at his side, and I turned on the vacuum in order to cover the noise. There was no way I was going to acknowledge either him or the TV, and so I kept my head down, reworking the same spot until my shoulder started to ache and I switched arms. *Just pretend it isn't happening,* I told myself, but this was unlike ignoring a subway car musician or a crazy stranger seated next to you at a restaurant counter. Like the cough of a sick person, Martin's efforts broadcast germs, a debilitating shame bug that traveled across the room in search of a new host. How terrible it is to be wrong, to go out on a limb and make an advance that isn't reciprocated. I thought of the topless stay-at-home wife, opening the door to the gay UPS driver, of all those articles suggesting you surprise that certain someone by serving dessert in the nude or offering up an unexpected striptease. They never tell you what to do should that someone walk out of the room or look at you with that mix of disgust and pity that ten, twenty, fifty years later will still cause you to burn every time you think about it. I've had some experience in this department, and Martin's depressing, wrongheaded display brought it all flooding back. I thought of the time . . . And of the time . . .

Whack, whack, whack. Whack, whack, whack.

It had now become the kind of masturbation that's an exercise in determination rather than pleasure. You'd give up but, godammit, you're the kind of person who carries a job through to the end, whether it's making a fool of yourself in front of a stranger or vacuuming somebody's living room. *I will finish this,* you think. *I will finish this.* And he did, eventually, climaxing with a bleak, long-winded moan. The paper at his elbow ceased its rattling, the video was turned off, and after pulling up his pants, he scooted into the bedroom. I didn't expect him to come back out and was surprised when he returned moments later with a stack of cash.

"You can stop vacuuming now," he said.

"But I'm not finished."

"I think you are," he said. Then he stepped closer and started handing me money. "Twenty, forty, sixty, eighty . . ." He counted softly, and with a different voice than he'd been using for the past two hours. This one was higher and passive, shaded with the kind of relief that follows a prolonged impersonation. "A hundred and ten, a hundred and twenty . . ." He counted to two hundred, which was over six times what I normally would have made. "Is that right?" he asked, and before I could answer, he topped the stack with a thirty-dollar tip.

"Let me ask you something," I said.

In recounting the rest of the story, it would be the next part that I could never get quite right, in part because it was so implausible but mainly because, between the blood taking and the five blankets, it was just too much. I assumed that Martin had learned about me from the *New York Times*, and he had. He'd read the article, written my name on a piece of paper, and looked me up in the phone book. He had also, it seemed, taken down the number of an erotic housecleaning service he'd found in the back of a porno magazine. The names and numbers had gotten confused, and he had phoned thinking that I was the sexpot. Such things happen, I guess, but you'd think that on seeing me, he might have realized his mistake. I've never dealt with an erotic housecleaning service, but something tells me the employees are hired for their looks rather than their vacuuming skills. Something tells me they only surface clean.

I'd wonder for weeks why Martin had put up with me. In his growing impatience, it seemed he would have simply told me what he wanted, but that would have required a different temperament, a straightforwardness that neither of us was capable of. In the phrase book of the indirect, "FIRE ISLAND" means "Let us masturbate together," while "Who does your mother love more?" translates to "I prefer to clean the kitchen in private, please." "I don't have a VCR" equals "Your behavior troubles me," and "You can always . . . you know" means "I think you should probably take your clothes off now." "What do you say we test your blood sugar" — that was just craziness talking.

After I'd collected my bag, Martin saw me to the door. "We'll have to do this again sometime," he said, meaning that we would never see each other again.

"That would be nice," I told him.

He offered his warm, gooey hand, and in a spirit of brotherhood, I accepted it.

The End of the Affair

On a summer evening in Paris, Hugh and I went to see *The End of the Affair,* a Neil Jordan adaptation of the Graham Greene novel. I had trouble keeping my eyes open because I was tired and not completely engaged. Hugh had trouble keeping his eyes open because they were essentially swollen shut: he sobbed from beginning to end, and by the time we left the theater, he was completely dehydrated. I asked if he always cried during comedies, and he accused me of being grossly insensitive, a charge I'm trying to plea-bargain down to simply obnoxious.

Looking back, I should have known better than to accompany Hugh to a love story. Such movies are always a danger, as unlike battling aliens or going undercover to track a serial killer, falling in love is something most adults have actually experienced at some point in their lives. The theme is universal and encourages the viewer to make a number of unhealthy comparisons, ultimately raising the question "Why can't *our* lives be like that?" It's a box best left unopened, and its avoidance explains the continued popularity of vampire epics and martial-arts extravaganzas.

The End of the Affair made me look like an absolute toad. The movie's voracious couple was played by Ralph Fiennes and Julianne Moore, who did everything but eat each other. Their love was doomed and clandestine, and even when the bombs were falling, they looked radiant. The picture was fairly highbrow, so I was surprised when the director employed a device most often seen in TV movies of the week: everything's going along just fine and then one of the characters either coughs or sneezes, meaning that within twenty minutes he or she will be dead. It might have been different had Julianne Moore suddenly started bleeding from the eyes, but coughing, in and of itself, is fairly pedestrian. When she did it, Hugh cried. When I did it, he punched me in the shoulder and told me to move. "I can't wait until she dies," I whispered. I don't know if it was their good looks or their passion, but something about Julianne Moore and Ralph Fiennes put me on the defensive.

I'm not as unfeeling as Hugh accuses me of being, but things change once you've

173

been together for more than ten years. They rarely make movies about long-term couples, and for good reason: our lives are boring. The courtship had its moments, but now we've become the predictable Part II no one in his right mind would ever pay to see. ("Look, they're opening their electric bill!") Hugh and I have been together for so long that in order to arouse extraordinary passion, we need to engage in physical combat. Once, he hit me on the back of the head with a broken wineglass, and I fell to the floor pretending to be unconscious. That was romantic, or would have been had he rushed to my side rather than stepping over my body to fetch the dustpan.

Call me unimaginative, but I still can't think of anyone else I'd rather be with. On our worst days, I figure things will work themselves out. Otherwise, I really don't give our problems much thought. Neither of us would ever publicly display affection; we're just not that type. We can't profess love without talking through hand puppets, and we'd never consciously sit down to discuss our relationship. These, to me, are good things. They were fine with Hugh as well, until he saw that damned movie and was reminded that he has other options.

The picture ended at about ten, and

afterward we went for coffee at a little place across the street from the Luxembourg Gardens. I was ready to wipe the movie out of my mind, but Hugh was still under its spell. He looked as though his life had not only passed him by but paused along the way to spit in his face. Our coffee arrived, and as he blew his nose into a napkin, I encouraged him to look on the bright side. "Listen," I said, "we maybe don't live in wartime London, but in terms of the occasional bomb scare, Paris is a pretty close second. We both love bacon and country music, what more could you possibly want?"

What more could he want? It was an incredibly stupid question and when he failed to answer, I was reminded of just how lucky I truly am. Movie characters might chase each other through the fog or race down the stairs of burning buildings, but that's for beginners. Real love amounts to withholding the truth, even when you're offered the perfect opportunity to hurt someone's feelings. I wanted to say something to this effect, but my hand puppets were back home in their drawer. Instead, I pulled my chair a few inches closer, and we sat silently at our little table on the square, looking for all the world like two people in love.

Repeat After Me

Although we'd discussed my upcoming visit to Winston-Salem, my sister and I didn't make exact arrangements until the eve of my arrival, when I phoned from a hotel in Salt Lake City.

"I'll be at work when you arrive," she said, "so I'm thinking I'll just leave the key under the hour ott near the ack toor."

"The what?"

"Hour ott."

I thought she had something in her mouth until I realized she was speaking in code.

"What are you, on a speakerphone at a methadone clinic? Why can't you just tell me where you put the goddam house key?"

Her voice dropped to a whisper. "I just don't know that I trust these things."

"Are you on a cell phone?"

"Of course not," she said. "This is just a regular cordless, but still, you have to be careful."

When I suggested that actually she *didn't*

have to be careful, Lisa resumed her normal tone of voice, saying, "Really? But I heard . . ."

My sister's the type who religiously watches the fear segments of her local Eyewitness News broadcasts, retaining nothing but the headline. She remembers that applesauce can kill you but forgets that in order to die, you have to inject it directly into your bloodstream. Pronouncements that cell-phone conversations may be picked up by strangers mix with the reported rise of both home burglaries and brain tumors, meaning that as far as she's concerned, all telecommunication is potentially life-threatening. If she didn't watch it on the news, she read it in *Consumer Reports* or heard it thirdhand from a friend of a friend of a friend whose ear caught fire while dialing her answering machine. Everything is dangerous all of the time, and if it's not yet been pulled off the shelves, then it's certainly under investigation — so there.

"Okay," I said. "but can you tell me *which* hour ott? The last time I was there you had quite a few of them."

"It's ed," she told me. "Well . . . edd*ish*."

I arrived at Lisa's house late the following afternoon, found the key beneath the flowerpot, and let myself in through the back door. A lengthy note on the coffee table explained how I might go about operating everything from the television to the waffle iron, each carefully detailed procedure ending with the line *"Remember to turn off and unplug after use."* At the bottom of page three, a postscript informed me that if the appliance in question had no plug — the dishwasher, for instance — I should make sure it had completed its cycle and was cool to the touch before leaving the room. The note reflected a growing hysteria, its subtext shrieking, *Oh-my-God-he's-going-to-be-alone-in-my-house-for-close-to-an-hour.* She left her work number, her husband's work number, and the number of the next-door neighbor, adding that she didn't know the woman very well, so I probably shouldn't bother her unless it was an emergency. "P.P.S. She's a Baptist, so don't tell her you're gay."

The last time I was alone at my sister's place she was living in a white-brick apartment complex occupied by widows and single, middle-aged working women. This was in the late seventies, when we were supposed to be living in dorms. College hadn't quite worked out the way she'd expected, and after two years in Virginia she'd returned to Raleigh and taken a job at a wineshop. It was a normal-enough life for a twenty-one-year-old, but being a dropout was not what she had planned for herself. Worse than that, it had not been planned *for* her. As children we'd been assigned certain roles — leader, bum, troublemaker, slut — titles that effectively told us who we were. As the oldest, smartest, and bossiest, it was naturally assumed that Lisa would shoot to the top of her field, earning a master's degree in manipulation and eventually taking over a medium-size country. We'd always known her as an authority figure, and while we took a certain joy in watching her fall, it was disorienting to see her with so little confidence. Suddenly she was relying on other people's opinions, following their advice and withering at the slightest criticism.

Do you really think so? Really? She was putty.

My sister needed patience and understanding, but more often than not, I found myself wanting to shake her. If the oldest wasn't who she was supposed to be, then what did it mean for the rest of us?

Lisa had been marked Most Likely to Succeed, and so it confused her to be ringing up gallon jugs of hearty burgundy. I had been branded as lazy and irresponsible, so it felt right when I, too, dropped out of college and wound up living back in Raleigh. After being thrown out of my parents' house, I went to live with Lisa in her white-brick complex. It was a small studio apartment — the adult version of her childhood bedroom — and when I eventually left her with a broken stereo and an unpaid eighty-dollar phone bill, the general consensus was "Well, what did you expect?"

I might reinvent myself to strangers, but to this day, as far as my family is concerned, I'm still the one most likely to set your house on fire. While I accepted my lowered expectations, Lisa fought hard to regain her former title. The wineshop was just a temporary setback, and she left shortly after becoming the manager. Photography interested her, so she taught herself to use a camera, ultimately landing a job in the photo department of a large international drug company, where she took pictures of germs, viruses, and people reacting to germs and viruses. On weekends, for extra money, she photographed weddings, which really wasn't that much of a stretch. Then she got married herself and quit the drug company in order to earn an English degree. When told there was very little call for thirty-page essays on Jane Austen, she got a real estate license. When told the housing market was down, she returned to school to study plants. Her husband, Bob, got a job in Winston-Salem, and so they moved, buying a new three-story house in a quiet suburban neighborhood. It was strange to think of my sister living in such a grown-up place, and I was relieved to find that neither she nor Bob particularly cared for it. The town was nice enough, but the house itself had a way of aging things. Stand outside and you looked, if not young, then at least relatively carefree. Step indoors and you automatically put on twenty years and a 401(k) plan.

My sister's home didn't really lend itself to snooping, and so I spent my hour in the kitchen, making small talk with Henry. It was the same conversation we'd had the last time I saw him, yet still I found it fascinating. He asked how I was doing, I said I was all right, and then, as if something might have drastically changed within the last few seconds, he asked again.

Of all the elements of my sister's adult

life — the house, the husband, the sudden interest in plants — the most unsettling is Henry. Technically he's a blue-fronted Amazon, but to the average layman, he's just a big parrot — the type you might see on the shoulder of a pirate.

"How you doing?" The third time he asked, it sounded as if he really cared. I approached his cage with a detailed answer, and when he lunged for the bars, I screamed like a girl and ran out of the room.

"Henry likes you," my sister said a short while later. She'd just returned from her job at the plant nursery and was sitting at the table, unlacing her sneakers. "See the way he's fanning his tail? He'd never do that for Bob. Would you, Henry?"

Bob had returned from work a few minutes earlier and immediately headed upstairs to spend time with his own bird, a balding green-cheeked conure named José. I'd thought the two pets might enjoy an occasional conversation, but it turns out they can't stand each other.

"Don't even *mention* José in front of Henry," Lisa whispered. Bob's bird squawked from the upstairs study, and the parrot responded with a series of high, piercing barks. It was a trick he'd picked up from Lisa's border collie, Chessie, and what was disturbing was that he sounded *exactly* like a dog. Just as, when speaking English, he sounded exactly like Lisa. It was creepy to hear my sister's voice coming from a beak, but I couldn't say it didn't please me.

"Who's hungry?" she asked.

"Who's hungry?" the voice repeated.

I raised my hand, and she offered Henry a peanut. Watching him take it in his claw, his belly sagging almost to the perch, I could understand what someone might see in a parrot. Here was this strange little fatso living in my sister's kitchen, a sympathetic listener turning again and again to ask, "So, really, how are you?"

I'd asked her the same question and she'd said, "Oh, fine. You know." She's afraid to tell me anything important, knowing I'll only turn around and write about it. In my mind, I'm like a friendly junkman, building things from the little pieces of scrap I find here and there, but my family's started to see things differently. Their personal lives are the so-called pieces of scrap I so casually pick up, and they're sick of it. More and more often their stories begin with the line "You have to swear you will never repeat this." I always promise, but it's generally understood that my word means nothing.

I'd come to Winston-Salem to address the students at a local college, and then again to break some news. Sometimes when you're stoned it's fun to sit around and think of who might play you in the movie version of your life. What makes it fun is that no one is actually going to make a movie of your life. Lisa and I no longer got stoned, so it was all the harder to announce that my book had been optioned, meaning that, in fact, someone was going to make a movie of our lives — not a student, but a real director people had actually heard of.

"A *what?*"

I explained that he was Chinese, and she asked if the movie would be in Chinese.

"No," I said, "he lives in America. In California. He's been here since he was a baby."

"Then what does it matter if he's Chinese?"

"Well," I said, "he's got . . . you know, a sensibility."

"Oh brother," she said.

I looked to Henry for support, and he growled at me.

"So now we have to be in a movie?" She picked her sneakers off the floor and tossed them into the laundry room. "Well," she said, "I can tell you right now that you are not dragging my bird into this." The movie was to be based on our pre-parrot years, but the moment she put her foot down I started wondering who we might get to play the role of Henry. "I know what you're thinking," she said. "And the answer is no."

Once, at a dinner party, I met a woman whose parrot had learned to imitate the automatic icemaker on her new refrigerator. "That's what happens when they're left alone," she'd said. It was the most depressing bit of information I'd heard in quite a while, and it stuck with me for weeks. Here was this creature, born to mock its jungle neighbors, and it wound up doing impressions of man-made kitchen appliances. I repeated the story to Lisa, who told me that neglect had nothing to do with it. She then prepared a cappuccino, setting the stage for Henry's pitch-perfect imitation of the milk steamer. "He can do the blender, too," she said.

She opened the cage door, and as we sat down to our coffees, Henry glided down onto the table. "Who wants a kiss?" She stuck out her tongue, and he accepted the tip gingerly between his upper and lower beak. I'd never dream of doing such a thing, not because it's across-the-board disgusting but because he would have bitten the shit out of me. Though Henry might occasionally fan his tail in my direction, it is understood that he is loyal to only one person, which, I think, is another reason my sister is so fond of him.

"Was that a good kiss?" she asked. "Did you like that?"

I expected a yes-or-no answer and was disappointed when he responded with the exact same question: "Did you like that?" Yes, parrots can talk, but unfortunately they have no idea what they're actually saying. When she first got him, Henry spoke the Spanish he'd learned from his captors. Asked if he'd had a good night's sleep, he'd say simply, *"Hola,"* or *"Bueno."* He goes through phases, favoring an often repeated noise or sentence, and then moving on to something else. When our mother died, Henry learned how to cry. He and Lisa would set each other off, and the two of them would go on for hours. A few years later, in the midst of a brief academic setback, she trained him to act as her emotional cheerleader. I'd call and hear him in the background, screaming, "We love you, Lisa!" and "You can do it!" This was replaced, in time, with the far more practical "Where are my keys?"

After finishing our coffees, Lisa and I drove to Greensboro, where I delivered my scheduled lecture. That is to say, I read stories about my family. After the reading, I answered questions about them, thinking all the while how odd it was that these strangers seemed to know so much about my brother and sisters. In order to sleep at night, I have to remove myself from the equation, pretending that the people I love expressly choose to expose themselves. Amy breaks up with a boyfriend and sends out a press release. Paul regularly discusses his bowel movements on daytime talk shows. I'm not the conduit, but just a poor typist stuck in the middle. It's a delusion much harder to maintain when a family member is actually *in* the audience.

The day after the reading, Lisa called in sick and we spent the afternoon running errands. Winston-Salem is a city of plazas — midsize shopping centers, each built around an enormous grocery store. I was looking for cheap cartons of cigarettes, so we drove from plaza to plaza, comparing prices and talking about our sister Gretchen. A year earlier she'd bought a pair of flesh-eating Chinese box turtles with pointed noses and spooky translucent skin. The two of them lived in an outdoor pen and were relatively happy until raccoons dug beneath the wire, chewing the front legs off the female and the rear legs off her husband.

"I may have the order wrong," Lisa said. "But you get the picture."

The couple survived the attack and continued to track the live mice that constituted their diet, propelling themselves forward like a pair of half-stripped Volkswagens.

"The sad part is that it took her two weeks to notice it," Lisa said. "Two weeks!" She shook her head and drove past our exit. "I'm sorry, but I don't know how a responsible pet owner could go that long without noticing a thing like that. It's just not right."

According to Gretchen, the turtles had no memories of their former limbs, but Lisa wasn't buying it. "Oh, come on," she said. "They must at least have phantom pains. I mean, how can a living creature not mind losing its legs? If anything like that happened to Chessie, I honestly don't know how I could live with myself." Her eyes misted and she wiped them with the back of her hand. "My little collie gets a tick and I go crazy."

Lisa's a person who once witnessed a car accident, saying, "I just hope there isn't a dog in the backseat." Human suffering doesn't faze her much, but she'll cry for days over a sick-pet story.

"Did you see that movie about the Cuban guy?" she asked. "It played here for a while but I wouldn't go. Someone told me a dog gets killed in the first fifteen minutes, so I said forget it."

I reminded her that the main character died as well, horribly, of AIDS, and she pulled into the parking lot, saying, "Well, I just hope it wasn't a *real* dog."

I wound up buying cigarettes at Tobacco USA, a discount store with the name of a theme park. Lisa had officially quit smoking ten years earlier and might have taken it up again were it not for Chessie, who, according to the vet, was predisposed to lung ailments. "I don't want to give her secondhand emphysema, but I sure wouldn't mind taking some of this weight off. Tell me the truth, do I look fat to you?"

"Not at all."

She turned sideways and examined herself in the front window of Tobacco USA. "You're lying."

"Well, isn't that what you want me to say?"

"Yes," she said. "But I want you to really mean it."

But I *had* meant it. It wasn't the weight I noticed so much as the clothing she wore to cover it up. The loose, baggy pants and oversize shirts falling halfway to her knees: This was the look she'd adopted a few months earlier, after she and her husband had gone to the mountains to visit Bob's parents. Lisa had been sitting beside the fire, and when she scooted her chair toward the center of the room, her father-in-law said, "What's the matter, Lisa? Getting too fat — I mean hot. Getting too hot?"

He tried to cover his mistake, but it was too late. The word had already been seared into my sister's brain.

"Will I have to be fat in the movie?" she asked.

"Of course not," I said. "You'll be just . . . like you are."

"Like I am according to who?" she

asked. "The Chinese?"

"Well, not *all* of them," I said. "Just one."

Normally, if at home during a weekday, Lisa likes to read nineteenth-century novels, breaking at one to eat lunch and watch a television program called *Matlock*. By the time we finished with my errands, the day's broadcast had already ended, and so we decided to go to the movies — whatever she wanted. She chose the story of a young Englishwoman struggling to remain happy while trying to lose a few extra pounds, but in the end she got her plazas confused, and we arrived at the wrong theater just in time to watch *You Can Count on Me*, the Kenneth Lonergan movie in which an errant brother visits his older sister. Normally, Lisa's the type who talks from one end of the picture to the other. A character will spread mayonnaise onto a chicken sandwich and she'll lean over, whispering, "One time, I was doing that? And the knife fell into the toilet." Then she'll settle back in her seat and I'll spend the next ten minutes wondering why on earth someone would make a chicken sandwich in the bathroom. This movie reflected our lives so eerily that for the first time in recent memory, she was stunned into silence. There was no physical resemblance between us and the main characters — the brother and sister were younger and orphaned — but like us, they'd stumbled to adulthood playing the worn, confining roles assigned to them as children. Every now and then one of them would break free, but for the most part they behaved not as they wanted to but as they were expected to. In brief, a guy shows up at his sister's house and stays for a few weeks until she kicks him out. She's not evil about it, but having him around forces her to think about things she'd rather not, which is essentially what family members do, at least the family members my sister and I know.

On leaving the theater, we shared a long, uncomfortable silence. Between the movie we'd just seen and the movie about to be made, we both felt awkward and self-conscious, as if we were auditioning for the roles of ourselves. I started in with some benign bit of gossip I'd heard concerning the man who'd played the part of the brother but stopped after the first few sentences, saying that, on second thought, it wasn't very interesting. She couldn't think of anything, either, and so we said nothing, each of us imagining a bored audience shifting in their seats.

We stopped for gas on the way home and were parking in front of her house when she turned to relate what I've come to think of as the quintessential Lisa story. "One time," she said, "one time I was out driving?" The incident began with a quick trip to the grocery store and ended, unexpectedly, with a wounded animal stuffed into a pillowcase and held to the tailpipe of her car. Like most of my sister's stories, it provoked a startling mental picture, capturing a moment in time when one's actions seem both unimaginably cruel and completely natural. Details were carefully chosen and the pace built gradually, punctuated by a series of well-timed pauses. "And then . . . and then . . ." She reached the inevitable conclusion and just as I started to laugh, she put her head against the steering wheel and fell apart. It wasn't the gentle flow of tears you might release when recalling an isolated action or event, but the violent explosion that comes when you realize that all such events are connected, forming an endless chain of guilt and suffering.

I instinctively reached for the notebook I keep in my pocket and she grabbed my hand to stop me. "If you ever," she said, "*ever* repeat that story, I will never talk to you again."

In the movie version of our lives, I would have turned to offer her comfort, reminding her, convincing her that the action she'd described had been kind and just. Because it was. She's incapable of acting otherwise.

In the *real* version of our lives, my immediate goal was simply to change her mind. "Oh, come on," I said. "The story's really funny, and, I mean, it's not like *you're* going to do anything with it."

Your life, your privacy, your occasional sorrow — it's not like you're going to do anything with it. Is this the brother I always was, or the brother I have become?

I'd worried that, in making the movie, the director might get me and my family wrong, but now a worse thought occurred to me: What if he got us right?

Dusk. The camera pans an unremarkable suburban street, moving in on a parked four-door automobile, where a small, evil man turns to his sobbing sister, saying, "What if I use the story but say that it happened to a friend?"

But maybe that's not the end. Maybe before the credits roll, we see this same man getting out of bed in the middle of the night, walking past his sister's room, and continuing downstairs into the kitchen. A switch is thrown, and we notice, in the far corner of the room, a large standing birdcage covered with a tablecloth. He approaches it carefully and removes the cloth, waking a blue-fronted Amazon parrot, its eyes glowing red in the sudden light. Through everything that's gone before this moment, we understand that the man has something important to say. From his own mouth the words are meaningless, and so he pulls up a chair. The clock reads three a.m., then four, then five, as he sits before the brilliant bird, repeating slowly and clearly the words "Forgive me. Forgive me. Forgive me."

Six to Eight Black Men

I've never been much for guidebooks, so when trying to get my bearings in some strange American city, I normally start by asking the cabdriver or hotel clerk some silly question regarding the latest census figures. I say "silly" because I don't really *care* how many people live in Olympia, Washington, or Columbus, Ohio. They're nice-enough places, but the numbers mean nothing to me. My second question might have to do with the average annual rainfall, which, again, doesn't tell me anything about the people who have chosen to call this place home.

What really interests me are the local gun laws. Can I carry a concealed weapon and, if so, under what circumstances? What's the waiting period for a tommy gun? Could I buy a Glock 17 if I were recently divorced or fired from my job? I've learned from experience that it's best to lead into this subject as delicately as possible, especially if you and the local citizen are alone and enclosed in a relatively small area. Bide your time, though, and you can walk away with some excellent stories. I've learned, for example, that the blind can legally hunt in both Texas and Michigan. In Texas they must be accompanied by a sighted companion, but I heard that in Michigan they're allowed to go it alone, which raises the question: How do they find whatever it is they just shot? In addition to that, how do they get it home? Are the Michigan blind allowed to drive as well? I ask about guns not because I want one of my own but because the answers vary so widely from state to state. In a country that's become increasingly homogeneous, I'm reassured by these last charming touches of regionalism.

Firearms aren't really an issue in Europe, so when traveling abroad, my first question usually relates to barnyard animals. "What do your roosters say?" is a good icebreaker, as every country has its own unique interpretation. In Germany, where dogs bark "vow vow" and both the frog and the duck say "quack," the rooster greets the dawn with a hearty "kik-a-riki." Greek roosters crow "kiri-a-kee," and in France they scream "coco-rico," which sounds like one of those horrible premixed cocktails with a pirate on the label. When told that an American rooster says "cock-a-doodle-doo," my hosts look at me with disbelief and pity.

"When do you open your Christmas presents?" is another good conversation starter, as I think it explains a lot about national character. People who traditionally open gifts on Christmas Eve seem a bit more pious and family-oriented than those who wait until Christmas morning. They go to Mass, open presents, eat a late meal, return to church the following morning, and devote the rest of the day to eating another big meal. Gifts are generally reserved for children, and the parents tend not to go overboard. It's nothing I'd want for myself, but I suppose it's fine for those who prefer food and family to things of real value.

In France and Germany gifts are exchanged on Christmas Eve, while in the Netherlands the children open their presents on December 5, in celebration of St. Nicholas Day. It sounded sort of quaint until I spoke to a man named Oscar, who filled me in on a few of the details as we walked from my hotel to the Amsterdam train station.

Unlike the jolly, obese American Santa, Saint Nicholas is painfully thin and dresses not unlike the pope, topping his robes with a tall hat resembling an embroidered tea cozy. The outfit, I was told, is a carryover from his former career, when he served as the bishop of Turkey.

"I'm sorry," I said, "but could you repeat that?"

One doesn't want to be too much of a cultural chauvinist, but this seemed completely wrong to me. For starters, Santa didn't *used to do* anything. He's not retired and, more important, he has nothing to do with Turkey. It's too dangerous there, and the people wouldn't appreciate him. When asked how he got from Turkey to the North Pole, Oscar told me with complete conviction that Saint Nicholas currently resides in Spain, which again is simply not true. Though he could probably live wherever he wanted, Santa chose the North Pole specifically because it is harsh and isolated. No one can spy on him, and he doesn't have to worry about people coming to the door. Anyone can come to the door in Spain, and in that outfit he'd most certainly be recognized. On top of that, aside from a few pleasantries, Santa doesn't speak Spanish. "Hello. How are you? Can I get you some candy?" Fine. He knows enough to get by, but he's not fluent and he certainly doesn't eat tapas.

While our Santa flies in on a sled, the Dutch version arrives by boat and then transfers to a white horse. The event is televised, and great crowds gather at the waterfront to greet him. I'm not sure if there's a set date, but he generally docks in late November and spends a few weeks hanging out and asking people what they want.

"Is it just him alone?" I asked. "Or does he come with some backup?"

Oscar's English was close to perfect, but he seemed thrown by a term normally reserved for police reinforcement.

"Helpers," I said. "Does he have any elves?"

Maybe I'm overly sensitive, but I couldn't help but feel personally insulted when Oscar denounced the very idea as grotesque and unrealistic. "Elves," he said. "They are just so silly."

The words *silly* and *unrealistic* were redefined when I learned that Saint Nicholas travels with what was consistently described as "six to eight black men." I asked several Dutch people to narrow it down, but none of them could give me an exact number. It was always "six to eight," which seems strange, seeing as they've had hundreds of years to get an accurate head count.

The six to eight black men were characterized as personal slaves until the mid-1950s, when the political climate changed and it was decided that instead of being slaves they were just good friends. I think history has proved that something usually comes *between* slavery and friendship, a period of time marked not by cookies and quiet hours beside the fire but by bloodshed and mutual hostility. They have such violence in the Netherlands, but rather than duking it out amongst themselves, Santa and his former slaves decided to take it out on the public. In the early years if a child was naughty, Saint Nicholas and the six to eight black men would beat him with what Oscar described as "the small branch of a tree."

"A switch?"

"Yes," he said. "That's it. They'd kick him and beat him with a switch. Then if the youngster was really bad, they'd put him in a sack and take him back to Spain."

"Saint Nicholas would *kick* you?"

"Well, not anymore," Oscar said. "Now he just *pretends* to kick you."

He considered this to be progressive, but in a way I think it's almost more perverse than the original punishment. "I'm going to hurt you but not really." How many times have we fallen for that line? The fake slap invariably makes contact, adding the elements of shock and betrayal to what had previously been plain old-fashioned fear. What kind of a Santa spends his time pretending to kick people before stuffing them into a canvas sack? Then, of course, you've got the six to eight former slaves who could potentially go off at any moment. This, I think, is the greatest difference between us and the Dutch. While a certain segment of our population might be perfectly happy with the arrangement, if you told the average white American that six to eight nameless black men would be sneaking into his house in the middle of the night, he would barricade the doors and arm himself with whatever he could get his hands on.

"*Six to eight,* did you say?"

In the years before central heating, Dutch children would leave their shoes by the fireplace, the promise being that unless they planned to beat you, kick you, or stuff you into a sack, Saint Nicholas and the six to eight black men would fill your clogs with presents. Aside from the threats of violence and kidnapping, it's not much different than hanging your stockings from the mantel. Now that so few people actually have a working fireplace, Dutch children are instructed to leave their shoes beside the radiator, furnace, or space heater. Saint Nicholas and the six to eight black men arrive on horses, which jump from the yard onto the roof. At this point I guess they either jump back down and use the door or stay put and vaporize through the pipes and electrical cords. Oscar wasn't too clear about the particulars, but really, who can blame him? We have the same problem with our Santa. He's supposed to use the chimney, but if you don't have one, he still manages to get in. It's best not to think about it too hard.

While eight flying reindeer are a hard pill to swallow, our Christmas story remains relatively dull. Santa lives with his wife in a remote polar village and spends one night a year traveling around the world. If you're bad, he leaves you coal. If you're good and live in America, he'll give you just about anything you want. We tell our children to be good and send them off to bed, where they lie awake, anticipating their great bounty. A Dutch parent has a decidedly hairier story to relate, telling his children, "Listen, you might want to pack a few of your things together before going to bed. The former bishop of Turkey will be coming tonight along with six to eight black men. They might put some candy in your shoes, they might stuff you into a sack and take you to Spain, or they might just pretend to kick you. We don't know for sure, but we want you to be prepared."

This is the reward for living in the Netherlands. As a child you get to hear this story, and as an adult you get to turn around and repeat it. As an added bonus, the government has thrown in legalized drugs and prostitution — so what's *not* to love about being Dutch?

Oscar finished his story just as we arrived at the station. He was an amiable guy — very good company — but when he offered to wait until my train arrived I begged off, claiming I had some calls to make. Sitting alone in the vast, vibrant terminal, surrounded by thousands of polite, seemingly interesting Dutch people, I couldn't help but feel second-rate. Yes, the Netherlands was a small country, but it had six to eight black men and a really good bedtime story. Being a fairly competitive person, I felt jealous, then bitter. I was edging toward hostile when I remembered the blind hunter tramping off alone into the Michigan forest. He may bag a deer, or he may happily shoot a camper in the stomach. He may find his way back to the car, or he may wander around for a week or two before stumbling through your back door. We don't know for sure, but in pinning that license to his chest, he inspires the sort of narrative that ultimately makes me proud to be an American.

Rooster at the Hitchin' Post

The night the rooster was born, my father slipped into my bedroom to personally deliver the news. I was eleven years old and barely awake, yet still I recognized this as a supreme masculine moment: the patriarch informing his firstborn son that another player was joining the team. Looking around my room, at the vase of cattails arranged just so beside the potpourri bowl, he should have realized it was not his team I was playing for. Not even a girl would have découpaged her own electrical sockets, but finding it too painful to consider, my father played through, going so far as to offer a plastic-wrapped cigar, the band reading it's a boy. He'd gotten one for each of us. Mine was made of chewing gum, and his was the real thing.

"I hope you're not going to smoke that in here," I said. "Normally I wouldn't mind, but I just Scotchgarded the drapes."

For the first six months, my brother, Paul, was just a blob, then a doll my sisters and I could diaper and groom as we saw fit. Dress him appropriately and it was easy to forget the tiny penis lying like a canned mushroom between his legs. Given some imagination and a few well-chosen accessories, he was Paulette, the pouty French girl; Paola, the dark-wigged *bambina* fresh from her native Tuscany; Pauline, the swinging hippie chick. As a helpless infant, he went along with it, but by the age of eighteen months he'd effectively dispelled the theory that a person can be made gay. Despite our best efforts, the cigar band had been right. Our brother was a boy. He inherited my sports equipment, still in its original wrapping, and took to the streets with actual friends, playing whatever was in season. If he won, great, and if he lost, big deal.

"But aren't you going to weep?" we'd ask him. "Not even a little?"

We tried explaining the benefits of a nice long cry — the release it offered, the pity it generated — and he laughed in our faces. The rest of us blubbered like leaky showerheads, but for him water production was limited to sweat and urine. His sheets might be wet, but the pillow would remain forever dry.

Regardless of the situation, for Paul it

was always all about the joke. A warm embrace, a heartfelt declaration of concern: in moments of weakness we'd fall for these setups, vowing later to never trust him again. The last time I allowed my brother to hug me, I flew from Raleigh to New York oblivious to the sign he'd slapped to the back of my sports coat, a nametag sticker reading, "Hello, I'm Gay." This following the hilarity of our mother's funeral.

When my sisters and I eventually left home, it seemed like a natural progression — young adults shifting from one environment to the next. While our departures had been relatively painless, Paul's was like releasing a domestic animal into the wild. He knew how to plan a meal but displayed a remarkable lack of patience when it came time for the actual cooking. Frozen dinners were often eaten exactly as sold, the Salisbury steak amounting to a stickless meat Popsicle. I phoned one night just as he was leaning a family pack of frozen chicken wings against the back door. He'd forgotten to defrost them and was now attempting to stomp the solid mass into three 6-inch portions, which he'd stack in a pile and force into his toaster oven.

I heard the singular sound of boot against crystallized meat and listened as my brother panted for breath. "Goddam . . . fucking . . . chicken . . . wings."

I called again the following evening and was told that after all that work, the chicken had been spoiled. It tasted like fish, so he threw it away and called it a night. A few hours later, having decided that spoiled chicken was better than no chicken at all, he got out of bed, stepped outside in his underpants, and proceeded to eat the leftovers directly from the garbage can.

I was mortified. "In your *underpants?*"

"Damned straight," he said. "I ain't getting dressed up to eat no *fish-assed*-tasting chicken."

I worried about my brother standing in his briefs and eating spoiled poultry by moonlight. I worried when told he'd passed out in a parking lot and awoken to find a stranger's initials written in lipstick on his ass, but I never worried he'd be able to make a living. He's been working for himself since high school and at the age of twenty-six had founded a very successful floor-sanding company. The physical work is demanding, but more tiring still are the nitpicky touch-ups, the billing and hiring, and endless discussions with indecisive clients. When asked how he manages to keep all those people happy, Paul credits the importance of compromise, explaining, "Sometimes you got to put that dick in your mouth and roll it around a little. Ain't no need to swallow nothing, you just got to play on it for a while. You know what I'm saying?"

"Well . . . *yeah.*"

At an age when the rest of us were barely managing to pay our own rent, he had bought a house. At thirty-two he sold it and traded up, moving into an established neighborhood inside the Raleigh beltline. Four bedrooms and the place was his, as were the trucks and sport-utility vehicles that spilled from the driveway and onto the lawn he paid to have mowed. All this from a business philosophy based on the art of a blowjob.

Paul referred to his house as "the home of a confused clown," but to the naked eye, the clown seemed absolutely sure of himself. There was the farting mound of battery-operated feces positioned on the mantel, the namesake rooster inlaid into the living-room floor, the bright-green walls, and musical butcher knives. "No confusion here," you'd say, tripping over a concrete alligator. It was an awfully big place for just one clown, so I was relieved when told that a girlfriend had moved in, accompanied by an elderly pug named Venus.

My brother was overjoyed. "You want to talk at her? Hold on while I put her on the phone."

I prepared myself for the voice of a North Carolina girlfriend, something like Paul's but lower, and heard instead what sounded like a handsaw methodically working its way through a tree trunk. It was Venus. Months later he put me on the phone with their new dog, a six-week-old Great Dane named Diesel. I spoke to the outdoor cats, the indoor cats, and the adopted piglet that seemed like a good idea until it began to digest solid food. They'd been living together for more than a year when I finally met the girlfriend, a licensed hairdresser named Kathy. Erase the tattoos and the nicotine patch and she resembled one of those tranquil Flemish Madonnas, the ubiquitous Christ child replaced by a hacking pug. Her grace, her humor, her fur-matted sweaters — we loved her immediately. Best of all, she was from the North, meaning that should she and Paul ever conceive a child, it stood a fifty-fifty chance of speaking understandable English.

They announced their engagement and designed a late-May wedding tailor-made to disappoint the Greeks. It would not take place at the Holy Trinity Church but at a hotel on the coast of North Carolina. The service would be performed by a psychic they'd found in the phone book, and the music provided by a DJ named J.D. who worked weekdays at the local state penitentiary.

"Oh, well," his godmother sighed. "I guess that's how the young people like to do it these days."

I flew in from Paris two days before the wedding and was sitting in my father's kitchen when Paul came to the door dressed in a suit and tie. A former high school classmate had committed suicide, and he'd dropped by the house on his way home from the funeral. Since I'd last seen him, my once slim brother had gained a good sixty pounds. Everything seemed proportionately larger, but the bulk seemed to have settled about his face and torso, leaving him with what he referred to as Dick Do disease. "My stomach sticks out further than my dick do."

The added weight had softened certain features and swallowed others altogether. His neck, for instance. Obscured now by a second chin, his head appeared to balance directly upon his shoulders, and he walked delicately, as if to keep it from rolling off. I told myself that if I looked at my brother differently, it was because of the suit, not the weight. He was a grown man now. He was going to get married, and therefore, he was a changed person.

He took a sip of my father's weak coffee and spit it back into the mug. "This shit's like making love in a canoe."

"Excuse me?"

"It's fucking near water."

Then again, I thought, *maybe it* is *just the weight.*

I drove to the coast early the next morning with Lisa and her husband, Bob. Being the oldest and the only one married, she'd bumped herself up a notch, assuming the dual roles of experienced older sister and designated mother of the groom. To mention Paul, Kathy, or even Atlantic Beach was to inspire an upwelling of tears, followed by a choked "I just never thought I would see this day." From Morehead City on, she pretty much cried nonstop, provoked by the landmarks of our youth. "Oh, the bridge! The pier! The midget golf course!"

Paul was to be married in what used to be the John Yancy but was currently called the Royal Pavilion. The remodeling had been extensive, and what had once been a modest oceanfront hotel now boasted reception rooms and a wedding gazebo. Waitresses wore bow ties and pushed the scampi, explaining that it was Italian. Had you spent the 1980s in a coma, you might have been impressed with the fake columns and pastel color schemes, but as it was, there was something sad and mallish about it.

While the ceremony would take place at the Royal Pavilion, guests would be staying next door at the Atlantis, a three-story motel essentially unchanged since the early space age. It's where we'd spent weekends as young adults, when trips *to* the beach became trips *at* the beach. Mushrooms, cocaine, acid, peyote: I'd never checked in without being, at the very least, profoundly stoned, and on arrival I was surprised to find the furniture actually standing still.

My brother had chosen the Atlantis not for its sentimental value but because it allowed the various family dogs. Paul's friends, a group the rest of us referred to as simply "the Dudes," had also brought their pets, which howled and whined and clawed at the sliding glass doors. This was what happened to people who didn't have children, who didn't even know people who had children. The flower girl was in heat. The rehearsal dinner included both canned and dry food, and when my brother proposed a toast to his "beautiful bitch," everyone assumed he was talking about the pug.

An hour before the wedding, the men in my family were scheduled to meet in Paul's room, no women or Dudes allowed. I went expecting a once-in-a-lifetime masculine moment, and looking back, that's probably what I got. While my room was immaculate, Paul's was dark and littered with bones, like the cave of an animal. He'd only arrived the previous afternoon, but already it looked as though he'd been living there for years, surviving on beer and the bodies of missing beachcombers. I spread out a newspaper and sat on the bed as my father, the best man, attached my brother's cummerbund. It was five o'clock on one of the most important days of their lives and both of them were watching TV. It was a cable news channel, a special report concerning a flood in one of those faraway towns senselessly built on the banks of an untrustworthy river. Citizens stacked sandbags on a retaining wall. A wheelbarrow floated down the suburban street. "And still," the announcer said, "still the rain continues to fall."

I'd heard once, maybe falsely, that when filming the movie *Gandhi*, the director had hired extras to play the roles of sandbags, that it had actually been cheaper than finding the real thing. It seemed like a worthy conversational icebreaker, but before I could finish the first sentence, my father told me to put a lid on it.

"We're trying to watch some TV here," he said. "Jesus, do you mind?" Over in the bridal suite, they were applying makeup and systematically crying it back off. Noteworthy things were being said, and I couldn't help but feel I was in the wrong room. My father turned my brother to face him and, with one eye on the television, began knotting his bow tie.

"Water like that will fuck the shit out of some hardwood floors," Paul said. "Those sons of bitches are looking at total replacements, I'll tell you what."

"Well, you're right about that." My father helped the groom into his jacket and turned to give the flood victims one last look. "All right," he said. "Let's get married."

It was a busy day at the Royal Pavilion. The five o'clock wedding had gotten off to a late start, and we watched from the sidelines as a Marine Corps chaplain finished marrying an attractive young couple in their early twenties. Lisa and Amy gave the relationship three years at the most. Gretchen and I put it closer to eighteen months, and Tiffany suggested that if we wanted the real answer, we should ask the psychic, who stood beside a scrub pine entertaining Paul's godmother. She was a tall, conservatively dressed woman with flesh-colored hair and matching fingernails. Sunglasses hung from a chain around her neck, and she wiped their lenses while reciting her credentials. It seemed that aside from her regular Friday-night tarot-card readings, she also cured cancer, diabetes, and heart disease by touching the sufferers in secret, hard-to-reach places. "I've had the gift since I was seven," she said. "And believe me, I am *very* good at what I do."

When it came to weddings, she psychically read the prospective bride and groom, divining their innermost selves and using her findings to tailor unique, personally significant vows.

"Well, I, for one, think that that is really beautiful," Lisa said.

"I know you do," the psychic said. "I know you do."

The marines filed out of the gazebo, and we moved in to take their seats. "Who does that woman think she is?" Lisa whispered. "I mean, come on, I was only trying to be polite."

"I know you were," I said. "I know you were."

J.D. the DJ was stuck in bridge traffic, so the ceremony commenced without the prerecorded wedding march. Lisa predictably started howling the moment the bride rounded the Coke machine and came into view on the arm of her father. The dogs followed suit, and determined not to join them, I looked beyond the psychic's shoulder, to a small patch of ocean visible through the trees. It was the place where, twenty-two years earlier, my brother had come very close to drowning. We'd been horsing around at high tide and looked up to find ourselves on the other side of the waves, drifting farther and farther from the hotel. It wasn't natural to be out that far, and so I swam for shore, thinking he was right behind me.

"Greetings, friends and family," the psychic said. *"We stand on . . ."* She looked at the bride, towering over my pint-size brother. *"We stand on tiptoes this afternoon to celebrate the love of . . . Paul and Kathy."*

He wasn't supposed to be out at that time of day, especially with me. "You wind him up," my mother said. "For God's sakes, just give it a rest." When accused of winding up my sisters, I'd always felt a hint of shame, but I liked the fact that I could adequately enthuse a twelve-year-old boy. As an older brother, it was my job, and I liked to think that I was good at it. I swam for what felt like the length of a pool, then stopped and turned around. But Paul wasn't there.

"This love cannot be bought . . . in a store," the psychic said. *"It cannot be found . . . under a tree, beneath a . . . shell, or even in a . . ."* You could see her groping for a possible hiding place. *"Even in a . . . treasure chest buried centuries ago on the . . . historic islands that surround us."*

A swell moved in, and my brother went under, leaving only his right arm, which waved the international sign language for "I am going to die now and it is all your fault." I headed back in his direction, trying to recall the water-safety class I'd taken years earlier at the country club. *Think,* I told myself. *Think like a man.* I tried to focus, but all that came to me was the instructor, an athletic seventeen-year-old named Chip Pancake. I remembered the spray of freckles on his broad, bronzed shoulders and my small rush of hope as he searched the assembled students for a resuscitation victim. *Oh, choose me,* I'd whispered. *Me! Over here.* I recalled the smell of hamburgers drifting from the clubhouse, the sting of the life jacket against my sunburned back, and the crushing disappointment I felt when Chip selected Patsy Pyle, who would later describe the experience as "life-changing." These are not the sorts of memories that save lives, so I abandoned the past and relied instead upon instinct.

"We ask that this marriage be blessed with as many graces as there are . . . grains of sand in the . . . ocean."

In the end, I just sort of grabbed Paul by the hair and yelled at him to lie flat. He vomited a mouthful of seawater, and together we kicked our way back to the beach, washing ashore a good half mile from the hotel. Lying side by side, catching our breath in the shallow surf, it seemed a moment in which something should be said, some declaration of relief and brotherly love.

"Listen," I started. "I just want you to know . . ."

"Fuck you," Paul had said to me.

"*I do*," Paul now said to Kathy.

"I just never thought I'd see this day," Lisa blubbered.

My brother kissed his bride, and the psychic looked out at her audience, nodding her head as if to say, "I knew that would happen."

Cameras clicked and a wind kicked up, blowing Kathy's veil and train straight into the air. Her look of surprise, his frantic embrace — in resulting photographs it would appear as if she'd dropped from the sky, caught at the last moment by someone who would now introduce himself as the luckiest man in the world.

At the reception my brother danced the worm, throwing himself on his belly as the Dudes chanted, "Party, fat man, party." My father delivered a brief, awkward speech while waving a rubber chicken and again the cameras flashed.

"I cannot believe you," I said. "A rubber *chicken?*"

He claimed he'd been unable to find a

rubber rooster, and I explained that that wasn't really the point. "Not everyone has the ability to improvise," I said. "Where were your notes? Why didn't you come to me for help?"

If I was hard on him, it was because I'd wanted to deliver the big speech. I'd been planning on it since Paul was a boy, but nobody had asked me. Now I'd have to wait until his funeral.

At one a.m. the room rental ended and plans were made to move the reception onto the beach. Kathy changed out of her gown while Paul and I took the dogs for a quick walk across the front lawn of the Atlantis. For the first time since the wedding we were alone, and I wanted to force a moment out of it. The operative word here, the source of the problem, is *force*. Because it never works that way. In trying to be memorable, you wind up sounding unspeakably queer, which may be remembered but never the way you'd hoped. My brother had spent his life saving me from such moments, and now he would do it again.

A light rain began to fall, and just as I cleared my throat, Venus squatted in the grass, producing a mound of peanut-size turds.

"Aren't you going to clean that up?" I asked.

Paul pointed to the ground and whistled for the Great Dane, which thundered across the lawn and ate the feces in one bite.

"Tell me that was an accident," I said.

"Accident, hell. I got this motherfucker *trained*," he said. "Sometimes he'll stick his nose to her ass and just eat that shit on tap."

I thought of my brother standing in his backyard and training a dog to eat shit and realized I'd probably continue thinking about it until the day I die. Forget the tears and brotherly speeches, this was the stuff that memories are made of.

The Great Dane licked his lips and searched the grass for more. "What was it you were going to say?" Paul asked.

"Oh, nothing."

From their perch atop an endangered dune, the Dudes emitted a war cry. Kathy called out from the door of her room, and together with his dogs, my brother set forth, spreading a love that could not be found under a tree, beneath a shell, or even in a treasure chest buried centuries ago on the historic islands that surrounded us.

Possession

"Finding an apartment is a lot like falling in love," the real estate agent told us. She was a stylish grandmother in severe designer sunglasses. Dyed blond hair, black stockings, a little scarf tied just so around the throat: for three months she drove us around Paris in her sports car, Hugh up front and me folded like a lawn chair into the backseat.

At the end of every ride I'd have to teach myself to walk all over again, but that was just a minor physical complaint. My problem was that I already loved an apartment. The one we had was perfect, and searching for another left me feeling faithless and sneaky, as if I were committing adultery. After a viewing, I'd stand in our living room, looking up at the high, beamed ceiling and trying to explain that the other two-bedroom had meant nothing to me. Hugh took the opposite tack and blamed our apartment for making us cheat. We'd offered, practically begged, to buy it, but the landlord was saving the place for his daughters, two little girls who would eventually grow to evict us. Our lease could be renewed for another fifteen years, but Hugh refused to waste his love on a lost cause. When told our apartment could never truly be ours, he hung up the phone and contacted the real estate grandmother, which is what happens when you cross him: he takes action and moves on.

The place was dead to him, but I kept hoping for a miracle. A riding accident, a playhouse fire: lots of things can happen to little girls.

When looking around, I tried to keep an open mind, but the more places we visited, the more discouraged I became. If the apartment wasn't too small, it was too expensive, too modern, too far from the center of town. I'd know immediately that this was not love, but Hugh was on the rebound and saw potential in everything. He likes a wreck, something he can save, and so he became excited when, at the end of the summer, the grandmother got a listing for what translated to "a nicely situated whorehouse." His feeling grew as we made our way up the stairs and blossomed when the door was unlocked and the smell of stagnant urine drifted into the hall. The former tenants had moved out, leaving clues to both their size and their temperament. Everything from the waist down was either gouged, splintered, or smeared with a sauce of blood and human hair. I found a tooth on the living-room floor, and what looked to be an entire fingernail glued with snot to the inside of the front door. Of course, this was just me: Mr. Bad Mouth. Mr. Negative. While I was searching for the rest of the body, Hugh was racing back and forth between the hole that was a kitchen and the hole that was a bathroom, his eyes glazed and dopey.

We'd shared this expression on first seeing the old apartment, but this time he was on his own, feeling something that I could not. I tried to share his enthusiasm — "Look, faulty wiring!" — but there was a hollowness to it, the sound of someone who was settling for something and trying hard to pretend otherwise. It wasn't a horrible place. The rooms were large and bright, and you certainly couldn't argue with the location. It just didn't knock me out.

"Maybe you're confusing love with pity," I told him, to which he responded, "If that's what you think, I really feel sorry for you."

The grandmother sensed my lack of enthusiasm and wrote it off as a failure of imagination. "Some people can see only what's in front of them," she sighed.

"Hey," I said, "I have" — and I said the dumbest thing — "I have powers."

She pulled the phone from her handbag. "Prove it," she said. "The owner has gotten three offers, and he's not going to wait forever."

If finding an apartment is like falling in love, buying one is like proposing on your first date and agreeing not to see each other until the wedding. We put in our bid, and when it was accepted I pretended to be as happy as Hugh and his bridesmaid, the grandmother. We met with a banker, and a lawyer we addressed as Master LaBruce. I hoped that one of them would put an end to this — deny us a mortgage, unearth a codicil — but everything moved according to schedule. Our master presided over the closing, and the following day the contractor arrived. Renovations began, and still I continued to browse the real estate listings, hoping something better might come along. I worried, not just that we'd chosen the wrong apartment but the wrong neighborhood, the wrong city, the wrong country. "Buyer's remorse," the grandmother said. "But don't worry, it's perfectly natural." *Natural.* A strange word when used by an eighty-year-old with an unlined face and hair the color of an American school bus.

Three months after moving in, we took a trip to Amsterdam, a city often recommended by the phrase "You can get so fucked-up there." I'd imagined Day-Glo bridges and canals flowing with bong water, but it was actually closer to a Brueghel painting than a Mr. Natural cartoon. We loved the lean brick buildings and the wispy sounds of bicycle tires on freshly fallen leaves. Our hotel overlooked the Herengracht, and on checking in, I started to feel that we'd made a terrible mistake. Why settle in Paris before first exploring the possibility of Amsterdam? What had we been thinking?

On our first afternoon we took a walk and came across the Anne Frank House, which was a surprise. I'd had the impression she lived in a dump, but it's actually a very beautiful seventeenth-century building right on the canal. Tree-lined street, close to shopping and public transportation: in terms of location, it was perfect. My months of house hunting had caused me to look at things in a certain way, and on seeing the crowd gathered at the front door, I did not think, *Ticket line,* but, *Open house!*

We entered the annex behind the famous bookcase, and on crossing the threshold, I felt what the grandmother had likened to being struck by lightning, an absolute certainty that this was the place for me. That it would be mine. The entire building would have been impractical and far too expensive, but the part where Anne Frank and her family had lived, their triplex, was exactly the right size and adorable, which is something they never tell you. In plays and movies it always appears drab and old ladyish, but open the curtains and the first words that come to mind are not "I still believe all people are really good at heart" but "Who do I have to knock off in order to get this apartment?" That's not to say that I wouldn't have made a few changes, but the components were all there and easy to see, as they'd removed the furniture and personal possessions that normally make a room seem just that much smaller.

Hugh stopped to examine the movie-star portraits glued to Anne Frank's bedroom wall — a wall that I personally would have knocked down — and I raced on to the bathroom, and then to the water closet with its delft toilet bowl looking for all the world like a big soup tureen. Next it was upstairs to the kitchen, which was eat-in with two windows. I'd get rid of the countertop and of course redo all the plumbing, but first I'd yank out the wood stove and reclaim the fireplace. "That's your focal point, there," I heard the grandmother saying. I thought the room beside the kitchen might be my office, but then I saw the attic, with its charming dormer windows, and the room beside the kitchen became a little leisure nook.

Now it was downstairs for another look at the toilet bowl, then back upstairs to reconsider the kitchen countertop, which, on second thought, I decided to keep. Or maybe not. It was hard to think with all these people coming and going, hogging the stairwell, running their mouths. A woman in a Disneyland sweatshirt stood in the doorway taking pictures of my sink, and I intentionally bumped her arm so that the prints would come out blurry and undesirable. "Hey!" she said.

"Oh, 'Hey' yourself." I was in a fever, and the only thing that mattered was this apartment. It wasn't a celebrity or a historical thing, not like owning one of Maria Callas's eyelashes or a pair of barbecue tongs once brandished by Pope Innocent XIII. Sure, I'd *mention* that I was not the first one in the house to ever keep a diary, but it wasn't the reason I'd fallen in love with the place. At the risk of sounding too koombaya, I felt as if I had finally come home. A cruel trick of fate had kept me away, but now I was back to claim what was rightfully mine. It was the greatest feeling in the world: excitement and relief coupled with the giddy anticipation of buying stuff, of making everything just right.

I didn't snap out of it until I accidentally passed into the building next door, which has been annexed as part of the museum. Above a display case, written across the wall in huge, unavoidable letters, was this quote by Primo Levi: "A single Anne Frank moves us more than the countless others who suffered just as she did but whose faces have remained in the shadows. Perhaps it is better that way. If we were capable of taking in all the suffering of all those people, we would not be able to live."

He did not specify that we would not be able to live *in her house*, but it was definitely implied, and it effectively squashed any fantasy of ownership. The added tragedy of Anne Frank is that she almost made it, that she died along with her sister just weeks before their camp was liberated. Having already survived two years in hiding, she and her family might have stayed put and lasted out the war were it not for a neighbor, never identified, who turned them in. I looked out the window, wondering who could have done such a thing, and caught my reflection staring back at me. Then, beyond that, across the way, I saw the most beautiful apartment.

Put a Lid on It

In a bathroom at La Guardia Airport I watched a man take a cell phone from his jacket pocket, step into an empty stall, and proceed to dial. I assumed he was going to pee and talk at the same time, but looking at the space beneath the door, I saw that his pants were gathered about his ankles. He was sitting on the toilet.

Most airport calls begin with geography. "I'm in Kansas City," people say. "I'm in Houston." "I'm at Kennedy." When asked where he was, the man on the phone said simply, "I'm at the airport, what do you think?" The sounds of a public toilet are not the sounds one would generally associate with an airport, at least not a secure airport, and so his "What do you think?" struck me as unfair. The person he was talking to obviously felt the same way. "What do you mean, 'What airport?' " the man said. "I'm at La Guardia. Now put me through to Marty."

A short while later I was in Boston. My

sister Tiffany met me in the lobby of my hotel and suggested we spend the rest of the afternoon at her place. The bellman hailed a cab, and as we got in I told her the story of the man at La Guardia. "I mean he actually placed a call *while sitting on the toilet!*"

Tiffany is big on rules but allows a pretty wide margin when it comes to mortal sin. Rape, murder, the abandonment of children: these are taken on a case-by-case basis. What riles her are the small things, and in denouncing them, she tends toward proclamations, most beginning with the words "A person doesn't." "A person doesn't just go around *making* things out of pinecones," she'll say, or, "A person doesn't use the word *weenie* when talking about a hot dog. It isn't cute. It isn't funny. It isn't done."

In telling Tiffany about the man on the toilet, I expected a certain degree of outrage. I expected a proclamation, but instead she said only, "I don't believe in cell phones."

"But you *do* believe in placing calls while sitting on the toilet?"

"Well, it's not a *belief*," she said. "But I mean, sure."

I thought again of the La Guardia bathroom. "But can't people guess what's going on? How do you explain the noise?"

My sister held an imaginary phone to her mouth. Then she scrunched up her face and adopted the strained, broken voice commonly associated with heavy lifting. "I say, 'Don't mind me. I'm just trying to get the . . . lid off this . . . jar.' "

Tiffany settled back against the seat, and I thought of all the times I had fallen for that line, all the times I had pictured her standing helpless in her kitchen. "Try tapping the lid against the countertop," I'd said, or, "Rinse it in hot water; that sometimes works."

Eventually, after much struggle, she would let out a breath. "There we go . . . I've got it now." Then she would thank me, and I would feel powerful, believing myself to be the only man on earth who could open a jar over the telephone. Appealing to my vanity was an old trick, but there was more to it than that. Tiffany is an excellent cook. Shortcuts don't interest her, so I'd always assumed that her jar held something she had preserved herself. Jam, maybe, or peaches. The lid released, I had imagined a sweet smell rising to meet her nose, and the sense of pride and accomplishment that ultimately comes from doing things "the ol' fashioned way." I had felt proud by extension, but now I just felt betrayed.

"Daddy's been thinking about things a little too hard," she said.

"Daddy?"

"Yeah," she said. "You."

"Nobody calls me Daddy."

"Mamma does."

This is her new thing. All men are called Daddy, and all women, Mamma. At the age of forty she talks like a farsighted baby.

My sister lives in Somerville, on the ground floor of a small two-story house. There's a chain-link fence separating the yard from the sidewalk, and a garage out back, where she keeps her bike and the homemade rickshaw she regularly attaches to her bike. It's a cumbersome, chariot-like thing, with a plywood body and two wheels taken from a scrapped ten-speed. There are a lot of rules involving the rickshaw, most decreeing what a person can and cannot do upon seeing it. Laughing is out, as are honking, pointing, and tugging at the corners of your eyes in an attempt to appear Chinese. This last one is a lot more popular than you might think, and it irritates Tiffany the most. She's become fiercely protective of the Chinese, especially her landlady, Mrs. Yip, who encourages her to defeat fat by rhythmically pummeling her thighs and stomach. Every morning my sister turns on the TV and stands in the living room, beating herself for half an hour. She claims that it keeps her in shape, but more likely it's the bicycle and towing that heavy rickshaw.

"She's got a beautiful voice," my father says. "I just wish to hell she'd *do* something with it."

Asked what that something might be, he says that she should put out an album.

"But she doesn't sing."

"Well, she *could.*" He speaks as if not releasing an album is just laziness on her part, as if people just walk in off the street, lay down a dozen or so tracks, and hand them over to eager radio stations. I've never heard Tiffany sing so much as "Happy Birthday," but when it comes to speaking, my father is right — she does have a beautiful voice. Even when she was a child it was smoky and full-bodied, lending even her most banal statements a cunning, slightly sexual undertone.

"A person needs to use their best assets," my father says. "If she doesn't want to put out an album, she could maybe be a receptionist. All she'd have to do is answer the damned phone."

But Tiffany isn't looking for career advice, especially from our father.

"I think she's happy doing what she's doing," I tell him.

"Oh, baloney."

When she was thirteen Tiffany got braces, and when she was fourteen she tried to remove them with a set of pliers. She was on the lam at the time, a runaway trying to distance herself from the class photo my parents had given the police. In trying to track down my sister, I spoke to one of her friends, a tough-looking girl who went by the name of Scallywag. She claimed to know nothing, and when I accused her of lying, she opened a Coke bottle with her teeth and spit the cap into her front yard. "Listen," I said, "I'm not the enemy." But she had heard stories, and knew not to trust me.

Following her capture, Tiffany was put in juvenile detention and then sent away to a school my mother had heard about on one of the afternoon talk shows. Punishment consisted of lying bellydown on the floor while a counselor putted golf balls into your open mouth. "Tough love" this was called. Basically the place just re-strained you until you were eighteen and allowed to run away legally.

After her release Tiffany became interested in baking. She attended a culinary institute in Boston and worked for many years in the sort of restaurant that thought it amusing to flavor brownies with tarragon and black pepper. It was cooking for people who read rather than ate, but it paid well and there were benefits. From midnight to dawn, Tiffany stood in the kitchen, sifting flour and listening to AM talk radio, which is either funny or spooky, depending on your ability to distance yourself from the callers. Tommy from Revere, Carol from Fall River: they are lonely and crazy. You are not. But the line blurs at four a.m. and disappears completely when you find yourself alone in a tall paper hat, adding fresh chives to buttercream icing.

"Do you mind if I smoke?" Tiffany asks our cabdriver, and before he can answer, her cigarette is lit. "You can have one, too, if you want," she tells him. "It won't bother me in the least." The man, who is Russian, smiles into the rearview mirror, revealing a mouthful of gold teeth.

"Whoa, Daddy. We know where *you*

239

bank," Tiffany says, and I start to wish that one of us knew how to drive. Like our mother, my sister can talk to anyone. Were I not here and were she in a position to afford a cab, she would undoubtedly be sitting up front, complimenting the man on his signaling abilities and then, just for good measure, making fun of his ID photo or the name printed beneath it. Growing up, she had a reputation for dishonesty, and her relentless, often inappropriate truth telling is, to her, a way of turning that around. "I'm not going to lie to you," she'll say, forgetting that another option is to simply say nothing.

As we cross from Cambridge into Somerville, Tiffany points out a few of the other places she's worked over the past fifteen years. The last was a traditional Italian bakery staffed by aging war veterans with names like Sal and Little Joey. Throughout the day they'd invent excuses to fondle her rear end or run a free hand across the front of her apron, and she let them do it because: "(a) It didn't physically hurt, (b) I was the only woman, so who else's ass were they going to grab? and (c) The boss let me smoke."

The money wasn't what she was used to, but still she stayed on for close to a year, until the owner announced he was going on vacation. His extended family was holding a reunion in Providence, so the bakery would close for the first two weeks of October and everyone would go without pay. Tiffany has no credit cards or long-distance service. All her money goes toward rent and cable, and so she spent her vacation in front of the TV, pounding her empty stomach and growing progressively angrier. At the end of the two weeks she returned to work and asked her boss if he'd enjoyed what she called "your little Woptoberfest." She's usually a pretty good judge of just how far she can push someone, but this time she miscalculated. We pass the bakery and she tosses her cigarette out the window. "Woptoberfest," she says. "I mean, how could someone *not* find that funny?"

After the Italians came the rickshaw and a return to the vampire hours she'd held years earlier at the fine bakery. These days while the rest of the world sleeps, my sister goes through their garbage. She carries a flashlight and a pair of rubber gloves and comes across a surprising number of teeth. "But none like yours," she says to our driver. "Most of the ones I find are false."

"Most?" I say.

She digs into her knapsack and hands me a few stray molars. One is small and clean, most likely a child's, while the other is king-size and looks like something pulled from the ground. I tap the larger one against the window, convinced that it must be made of plastic. "Who would throw away a real tooth?" I ask.

"Not me," says the driver, who's been in and out of the conversation ever since Tiffany gave him permission to smoke.

"Yeah," she says. "Well, we know about *you*. Anyone else, though, anyone *American*, would say their good-byes and toss it. In this country, once something's out of your mouth, it's garbage, Daddy."

In addition to the teeth, my sister finds anniversary cards and ceramic ponies. Angry letters written but not sent to congressmen. Underpants. Charm bracelets. Small items are stuffed into her knapsack, and everything else goes into the rickshaw and, subsequently, her apartment. Someone dies and she'll make three or four trips in a single evening, carting away everything from armchairs to wastepaper baskets.

"Last week I found a turkey," she tells us.

I wait, thinking this is only half of the

sentence "I found a turkey . . . made of papier-mâché. I found a turkey . . . and buried it in the yard." When it becomes clear that there is no part two, I start to worry. "What do you mean, you *found* a turkey?"

"Frozen," she says. "In the trash."

"And what did you do with it?"

"Well, what do most people do with a turkey?" she says. "I cooked it and then I ate it."

This is a test, and I fail, saying all the boring things you might expect of the comfortable: That the turkey was undoubtedly thrown away for a good reason. That it had possibly been recalled, like a batch of tainted fish sticks. "Or maybe someone tampered with it."

"Who would intentionally fuck with a frozen turkey?" she asks.

I try envisioning such a person, but nothing comes. "Okay, maybe it had thawed and been refrozen. That's dangerous, right?"

"Listen to you," she says. "If it didn't come from Balducci's, if it wasn't raised on polenta and wild baby acorns, it has to be dangerous."

That's not what I meant at all, but just as I try to explain myself, she places her hand on the driver's shoulder. "If someone offered you a perfectly good turkey, you'd take it, wouldn't you?"

The man says yes, and she pats him on top of the head. "Mamma likes you," she says.

She's gotten him on her side, but unfairly, and I'm surprised by the degree to which it enrages me. "There's a difference between someone offering you 'a perfectly good turkey' and finding a turkey in a garbage can," I say.

"Trash can," she corrects me. "God, you make it sound as if I'm back behind the Star Market, burrowing through their Dumpster. It was just one turkey. Ease up, will you."

She has, of course, found valuable things as well and formed relationships with the sort of people who are wont to buy them. These are the guys you see at flea markets, men with beards and longish fingernails who scold should you refer to a certain color of Fiesta ware as "orange" rather than "red." There's something about them I don't trust, but when asked for a reason, I'm hard-pressed to come up with anything beyond their general unfamiliarity. When meeting a friend of Amy's or Lisa's, I feel a sense of recognition, but the people whom Tiffany hangs out with are a completely different breed. I'm thinking of the woman who was shot seven times while evading the police. She's lovely, really, but *evading the police?* As my brother would say, "That's some outlaw shit."

The closer we get to her apartment, the more my sister engages the cabdriver, and by the time he pulls in front of the house I am left out of the conversation completely. It seems the guy's wife had a hard time adjusting to life in the United States and has recently returned to her village outside of St. Petersburg.

"But you're not *divorced*," Tiffany says. "You still love her, right?"

On paying the man, I sense that she would be much more comfortable were he the guest instead of me. "Would you like to come in and use the bathroom?" she asks him. "Do you have any local calls you need to make?" He politely declines the invitation, and her shoulders slump as he pulls away from the curb. He was a nice-enough guy, but more than his friendship she'd wanted a buffer, someone to stand between herself and what she sees as my inevitable judgment. We climb the few steps to her porch and she hesitates before pulling the keys from her pocket. "I haven't had a chance to clean," she says, but the lie feels uncomfortable, and so she corrects herself. "What I meant to say is that I don't give a fuck what you think of my apartment. I didn't really want you here in the first place."

I'm supposed to feel good that Tiffany has gotten this off her chest, but first I need to make it stop hurting. Were I to ask, my sister would tell me exactly how much she has been dreading my visit, and so I don't ask and comment instead on the cat brushing its big rusty head against the porch rails. "Oh," she says. "That's Daddy." Then she slips off her shoes and opens the door.

The apartment I imagine during our phone calls is not the apartment that Tiffany actually inhabits. It's the same physical area, but I prefer to envision it as it was years ago, back when she held an actual job. It was never extravagant, never self-consciously decorated, but it was clean and comfortable and seemed like a nice place to come home to. There were curtains on the windows, and a second bedroom made up for guests. Then she got the rickshaw, and as her house became a revolving junk shop, she shed all traces of sentimentality. Things come in, and as rent time nears, they go out, the found kitchen table sold alongside the serving bowl once belonging to our great-aunt or the Christmas present you'd given her the year before. For a time certain objects were replaced, but then she hit a rough patch and learned to do without such things as chairs and lampshades. It is this absence I try to ignore on entering her apartment, and I do pretty well until we hit the kitchen.

The last time I visited, Tiffany was pulling up the linoleum. I'd assumed that this was part of a process, phase one to be followed by phase two. It hadn't occurred to me that this was a one-step procedure, the final product a tar-paper floor. Combine it with bare feet and you're privy to the pedicurist's worst nightmare. My sister has appendages connected to her ankles. They feature toes and arches, but I cannot call them feet. In color they resemble the leathery paws of great apes, but in texture they are closer to hooves. In order to maintain her balance, she'll periodically clear the bottoms of debris — a bottle cap, bits of broken glass, a chicken bone — but within moments she'll have stepped on something else and begun the process all over again. It's what happens when you sell both your broom and your vacuum cleaner.

I see the dirty rag covering the lower half of the kitchen window, the crusted broken-handled pans scattered across the greasy stovetop. My sister is living in a Dorothea Lange photograph, and the homosexual in me wants to get down on my knees and scrub until my fingers bleed. I'd done it on all my previous visits, hoping each time that it might make some kind of a lasting impression. Gleaming appliances, a bathroom reeking of bleach: "Doesn't this smell great!" I'd say. The last time I was here, after scraping, cleaning, and waxing her living-room floor, I watched as she overturned a wineglass onto what amounted to six hours' worth of work. It wasn't an accident, but a deliberate statement: I do not want what you have to offer. She later phoned my brother, referring to me as Fairy Poppins, which wouldn't bother me if it weren't so apt. I am determined not to get involved this time, but without the cleaning, I have no purpose and don't know what to do with myself.

"We could *talk*," Tiffany says. "That's something we've never tried."

Haven't we? I think. If I talk to Tiffany less than to my other sisters, it's because she never comes home. We spent months persuading her to attend my brother's wedding, and even when she agreed, we didn't really expect her to show up. She and Paul get along very well, but as a group the family makes her nervous. We're the ones who idly sat by while she was having golf balls putted into her mouth, and the less time she spends with us, the happier she is. "Don't you get it?" she says. "I don't *like* you people." *You people.* As if we're a collection agency.

Tiffany stomps her lit cigarette onto the tar-paper floor, and as she sits on the countertop I notice the smoldering butt still clinging to the bottom of her right hoof. "I've been doing a lot of tile work," she tells me, and I follow her finger in the direction of the refrigerator, where a mosaic panel leans against the wall. She started making them a few years ago, using the bits of broken crockery she finds in the trash. Her latest project is the size of a bath mat and features the remains of a Hummel figurine, the once cherubic face now reeling in a vortex of shattered coffee mugs. Like the elaborate gingerbread houses she made during her baking days, Tiffany's mosaics reflect the loopy energy of someone who will simply die if she doesn't express herself. It's a rare quality, and because it requires an absolute lack of self-consciousness, she is unable to see it.

"A woman offered to buy it," she tells me, genuinely surprised that someone might take an interest. "We set a price, but then, I don't know, I feel wrong accepting that kind of money."

I can understand thinking that you're not good enough, but no one needs cash more than Tiffany. "You could sell it and buy a vacuum cleaner," I say. "Lay some new linoleum on the floor, wouldn't that be nice?"

"What is it with you and my kitchen floor?" she asks. "Who cares about the goddam linoleum?"

In the corner of the room Daddy approaches my sports coat, kneading it with his paws before lying down and curling into a ball. "I don't know why I even bother with you," Tiffany says. She'd wanted to show me her artwork — something that truly interests her, something she's good at — and instead, like my father, I'm suggesting she become an entirely different person. Looking at her face, that combination of fatigue and defiance, I am reminded of a conversation I annually hold with my friend Ken Shorr.

ME: Did you get your tree yet?

KEN: I'm a Jew, I don't decorate Christmas trees.

ME: So you're going to go with a wreath instead?

KEN: I just told you, I'm a Jew.

ME: Oh, I get it. You're looking for a cheap wreath.

KEN: I'm not looking for a wreath at all. Leave me alone, will you.

ME: You're probably just tense because you haven't finished your Christmas shopping.

KEN: I don't Christmas shop.

ME: What are you telling me? That you *make* all of your presents?

KEN: I don't give Christmas presents *period*. Goddamit, I told you, I'm a *Jew*.

ME: Well, don't you at least need to buy something for your parents?

KEN: They're Jews, too, idiot. That's what makes *me* one. It's hereditary. Do you understand?

ME: Sure.

KEN: Say the words "I understand."

ME: I understand. So where are you going to hang your stocking?

I can't seem to fathom that the things

important to me are not important to other people as well, and so I come off sounding like a missionary, someone whose job it is to convert rather than listen. *"Yes, your Tiki god is very handsome, but we're here to talk about Jesus."* It's no wonder Tiffany dreads my visits. Even when silent, I seem to broadcast my prissy disapproval, comparing the woman she is with the woman she will never be, a sanitized version who struggles with real jars and leaves other people's teeth and frozen turkeys where she finds them. It's not that I don't like her — far from it — I just worry that, without a regular job and the proper linoleum, she'll fall through a crack and disappear to a place where we can't find her.

The phone rings in the living room and I'm not surprised when Tiffany answers it. She does not tell her caller that she has company, but rather, much to my relief, she launches into what promises to be a long conversation. I watch my sister pace the living room, her great hooves kicking up clouds of dust, and when I am certain she's no longer looking, I shoo Daddy off my sports coat. Then I fill the sink with hot, soapy water, roll up my shirtsleeves, and start saving her life.

A Can of Worms

Hugh wanted hamburgers, so he, his friend Anne, and I went to a place called the Apple Pan. This was in Los Angeles, a city I know nothing about. The names of certain neighborhoods are familiar from watching TV, but I don't understand what it means to be in Culver City as opposed to, say, Silver Lake or Venice Beach. Someone suggests a destination and I just sort of go along and wait to be surprised.

I thought the Apple Pan would be a restaurant, but it was more like a diner — no tables, just stools arranged along a U-shaped counter. We ordered our hamburgers from a man in a paper hat, and while waiting for them to arrive, Anne pulled out some pictures of her bull terrier. She's a professional photographer, so they were portraits rather than snapshots. Here was the dog peeking out from behind a curtain. Here was the dog sitting human-style in an easy chair, a paw resting on the paunch of his stomach. Gary, I think his name was.

When she's not taking pictures of her dog, Anne flies around the country, on assignment for various magazines. A day earlier she'd returned from Boston, where she photographed a firefighter whose last name is Bastardo. "That's *bastard* with an *o* on the end," she said. "Don't you think that's funny?"

Hugh told her about some neighbors in Normandy whose last name translates to "hot ass," but unless you speak French, it's hard to get the joke.

"Is that hyphenated?" Anne asked. "I mean, did Miss Hot marry Mr. Ass, or is it all one word?"

"One word," Hugh said.

Thinking the conversation would rest there for a while, I prepared myself to contribute, wary of how easy it is to fall into a game of one-upmanship. If you know a Candy Dick, the other person is bound to know a Harry Dick or a Dick Eader. I'd recently learned of the race-car driver Dick Trickle, but for the time being we were operating on a higher plane, and so I mentioned Bronson Charles, a woman I'd met earlier that week in Texas. Had she been young, I would have wondered, not about her but about her parents, who obviously thought they were being clever. But

Bronson Charles was in her seventies and had married into the last name. It wasn't funny, just odd — the well-bred matron and the action hero, their sexes, names, and natures reversed. It was like meeting a timid man named Taylor Elizabeth.

Anne and Hugh met in college, and when our hamburgers arrived they reminisced about some of the people they had gone to school with. "What was that guy's name? I think he was in the Art Department, Mike, maybe, or Mark. He used to go out with Karen, I think her name was. Or Kimberly. You know who I mean."

Talk like this can go on for hours, and while you do have to accept it, you don't have to actually pay attention. I stared straight ahead, watching a broken-nosed cook top a hamburger with cheese, and then I turned slightly to my left and began listening to the two men seated on the other side of me. There was about them the weariness of people who could not afford to retire and would keep on toiling, horselike, until they dropped. The man beside me wore a T-shirt endorsing the state of Florida, and as if the weather were completely different on the other side of the ketchup bottle, the man beside him wore a thick wool sweater and heavy corduroy pants. A coat rested in his lap, and before him, on the counter, sat a newspaper and an empty cup of coffee. "Did you read about those worms?" he asked.

He was referring to the can of nematodes — tiny worms — recently discovered on the Texas plains. They'd been sent up with the doomed space shuttle and had somehow managed to survive the explosion, the cause of which was still a mystery. The man in the sweater massaged his chin and stared into space. "I've been thinking we could solve this problem in no time," he said. "If only . . . if only we could get the damned things to talk."

It sounded crazy but I remember thinking the same thing about the Akita in the O.J. Simpson case. *"Put it on the stand. Let's hear what it's got to say."* It was one of those ideas that, just for a second, seemed entirely logical, the one solution that nobody else had thought of.

The man in the T-shirt considered the possibility. "Well," he said, "even if the worms *could* talk, it wouldn't do much good. They was in that can, remember?"

"I guess you're right."

The men stood to pay their bills, and before they reached the door their stools were taken by two people who did not know each other. One was a man dressed in a fine suit, and the other a young woman who sat down and immediately started reading what looked to be a script. Over on my right Hugh had decided that rather than Karen or Kimberly, their classmate had been named Katherine. While I'd been listening to my neighbors, Anne had ordered me a slice of pie, and as I picked up my fork she told me that I was supposed to eat it backward, starting with the outer crust and working my way inward. "Your last bite should be the point, and you're supposed to make a wish on it," she said. "Hasn't anyone ever told you that?"

"Come again?"

She looked at me the way you might at someone who regularly tosses money into the fire. The senselessness! The waste! "Well, better late than never," she said, and repositioned my plate.

As Anne and Hugh resumed their conversation, I thought of all the pie I had eaten during the course of my life, and wondered how different things might be if only I had wished upon the points. To begin with, I would not be seated at the Apple Pan, that much was certain. Had I gotten my wish at the age of eight, I would still be rounding up mummies in Egypt, luring them from their tombs and trapping them in heavy iron cages. All subsequent wishes would have been based upon the life I had already established: a new set of boots, a finer whip, greater command of the mummy language. That's the problem with wishes, they ensnare you. In fairy tales they're nothing but trouble, magnifying the greed and vanity of the person for whom they are granted. One's best bet — and the moral to all those stories — is to be unselfish and make your wish for the benefit of others, trusting that their happiness will make you happy as well. It's a nice idea but would definitely take some getting used to.

Since we'd entered, the Apple Pan had grown progressively busier. All the seats were now taken, and people leaned against the wall, their eyes moving from stool to stool, determining which customers should pay up and get out. Looking around, I saw that we were the likeliest candidates. The man in the paper hat had removed our hamburger wrappers, and all that remained was a single plate, supporting the tip of my pie. I wished that the people against the wall would stop staring at us, and then quickly, but not quick enough, I tried to take it back.

"I guess we should get going," Hugh said, and he and Anne pulled out their wallets. There was a little struggle over who would pay — "It's my treat," "No, it's mine" — but I stayed out of it, thinking of what might have been had I not wasted my wish. A laboratory filled with sensitive equipment. Men in white coats, trembling with hope and wonder as they lean forward, catching the sound of one small voice. "Come to think of it," the worm says, "I *do* remember seeing something suspicious."

Chicken in the Henhouse

It was one of those hotels without room service, the type you wouldn't mind if you were paying your own bill but would complain about if someone else was paying. I was not paying my own bill, and so the deficiencies stuck out and were taken as evidence of my host's indifference. There was no tub, just a plastic shower stall, and the soap was brittle and smelled like dishwashing detergent. The bedside lamp was missing a bulb, but that could have been remedied easily enough. I could have asked for one at the front desk, but I didn't want a lightbulb. I just wanted to feel put-upon.

It started when the airline lost my luggage. Time was lost filling out forms, and I'd had to go directly from the airport to a college an hour north of Manchester, where I gave a talk to a group of students. Then there was a reception and a forty-five-minute drive to the hotel, which was out in the middle of nowhere. I arrived at one a.m. and found they had booked me into a basement room. Late at night it didn't much matter, but in the morning it did. To open the curtains was to invite scrutiny, and the people of New Hampshire stared in without a hint of shame. There wasn't much to look at, just me, sitting on the edge of the bed with a phone to my ear. The airline had sworn my suitcase would arrive overnight, and when it didn't, I called the 800 number printed on the inside of my ticket jacket. My choices were either to speak to a machine or to wait for an available human. I chose the human, and after eight minutes on hold I hung up and started looking for someone to blame.

"I don't care if it's my son, my congressman, what have you. I just don't approve of that lifestyle." The speaker was a woman named Audrey who'd called the local talk-radio station to offer her opinion. The Catholic Church scandal had been front-page news for over a week, and when the priest angle had been exhausted, the discussion filtered down to pedophilia in general and then, homosexual pedophilia, which was commonly agreed to be the worst kind. It was, for talk radio, one of those easy topics, like tax hikes or mass murder. "What do you think of full-grown men practicing sodomy on children?"

"Well, I'm *against* it!" This was always said as if it was somehow startling, a minority position no one had yet dared lay claim to.

I'd been traveling around the country for the past ten days, and everywhere I went I heard the same thing. The host would congratulate the caller on his or her moral fortitude, and wanting to feel that approval again, the person would rephrase the original statement, freshening it up with an adverb or qualifier. "Call me old-fashioned, but I just hugely think it's wrong." Then, little by little, they'd begin interchanging the words *homosexual* and *pedophile*, speaking as if they were one and the same. "Now they've even got them on TV," Audrey said. "And in the schools! Talk about the proverbial chicken in the henhouse."

"Fox," the host said.

"Oh, they're the worst," Audrey said. "*The Simpsons* and such — I never watch that station."

"I meant in the henhouse," the host said. "I believe the saying is 'the fox in the henhouse,' not 'the chicken in the henhouse.'"

Audrey regrouped. "Did I say chicken? Well, you get my point. These homosexuals can't reproduce themselves, and so they go into the schools and try to recruit our young people."

It was nothing I hadn't heard before, but I was crankier than usual and found myself in the middle of the room, one sock on and one sock off, shouting at the clock radio. "Nobody recruited *me,* Audrey. And I *begged* for it."

It was *her* fault I was stuck in a basement room with no luggage, her and all the people just like her: the satisfied families trotting from the parking lot to the first-floor restaurant, the hotel guests with whirlpool baths and rooms overlooking the surrounding forest. *Why waste the view on a homosexual? He only looks at schoolboys' rectums. And a suitcase? Please! We all know what they do with those.* They might not have come out and said it, but they were sure thinking it. I could tell.

It stood to reason that if the world was conspiring against me, my Mr. Coffee machine was broken. It sat on the bathroom counter, dribbling cold water, and after a brief, completely unsatisfying cry, I finished getting dressed and left the room. There was a staircase at the end of the hall, and beside it a little cleared area where a dozen or so elderly women knelt upon the carpet, piecing together a patchwork quilt. They looked up as I passed, one of them turning to ask me a question. "Yoin' shurch?" Her mouth was full of pins and it took me a moment to realize what she was saying — You going to church? It was an odd question, but then I remembered that it was a Sunday, and I was wearing a tie. Someone at the college had loaned it to me the night before, and I'd put it on in hopes it might distract from my shirt, which was wrinkled and discolored beneath the arms. "No," I told her, "I am *not* going to church." Oh, I was in a horrible mood. Midway up the stairs I stopped and turned back around. "I *never* go to church," I said. "Never. And I'm not about to start *now*."

"Shute shelf," she said.

Past the restaurant and gift shop, in the center of the lobby, was a complimentary beverage stand. I thought I'd get a coffee and take it outdoors, but just as I approached, a boy swooped in and began mixing himself a cup of hot chocolate. He looked like all of the kids I'd been seeing lately, in airports, in parking lots: the oversize sweatshirts stamped with team emblems, the baggy jeans and jazzy sneakers. His watch was fat and plastic, like a yo-yo strapped to his wrist, and his hair looked as if it had been cut with the lid of a can, the irregular hanks stiffened with gel and coaxed to stand at peculiar angles.

It was a complicated business, mixing a cup of hot chocolate. You had to spread the powdered cocoa from one end of the table to the other and use as many stirrers as possible, making sure to thoroughly chew the wetted ends before tossing them upon the stack of unused napkins. This is what I like about children: complete attention to one detail and complete disregard of another. When finally finished, he scooted over to the coffee urn, filling two cups, black, and fitting them with lids. The drinks were stacked into a tower, then tentatively lifted off the table. "Whoa," he whispered. Hot chocolate seeped from beneath the lid of the bottom cup and ran down his hand.

"Do you need some help with those?" I asked.

The boy looked at me for a moment. "Yeah," he said. "Carry these upstairs." There was no *please* or *thank you*, just "I'll take the hot chocolate myself."

He set the coffees back on the table, and as I reached for them it occurred to me that maybe this was not such a good idea. I was a stranger, an admitted homosexual traveling through a small town, and he was, like, ten. And alone. The voice of reason whispered in my ear. *Don't do it, buster. You're playing with fire.*

I withdrew my hands, then stopped, thinking, *Wait a minute. That's not reason. It's Audrey, that crackpot from the radio.* The real voice of reason sounds like Bea Arthur, and when it failed to pipe up, I lifted the coffees off the table and carried them toward the elevator, where the boy stood mashing the call button with his chocolate-coated fingers.

A maid passed and rolled her eyes at the desk clerk. "Cute kid."

Before the church scandal I might have said the same thing, only without the sarcasm. Now, though, any such observation seemed suspect. Though Audrey would never believe it, I am not physically attracted to children. They're like animals to me, fun to watch but beyond the bounds of my sexual imagination. That said, I am a person who feels guilty for crimes I have not committed, or have not committed in years. The police search the train station for a serial rapist and I cover my face with a newspaper, wondering if maybe I did it in my sleep. The last thing I stole was an eight-track tape, but to this day I'm unable to enter a store without feeling like a shop-lifter. It's all the anxiety with none of the free stuff. To make things just that much worse, I seem to have developed a remark-able perspiration problem. My conscience is cross-wired with my sweat glands, but there's a short in the system and I break out over things I didn't do, which only makes me look more suspect. Innocently helping to lighten a child's burden was a *good* thing — I knew this — yet moments after lifting the coffees off the table I was soaking wet. As usual, the sweat was fiercest on my forehead, under my arms, and, cruelly, on my ass, which is a great mystery to me. If the stress is prolonged, I'll feel the droplets inching down the back of my legs, trapped, finally, by my socks, which are cotton and bought expressly for their absorbent powers.

If there was a security camera in the lobby, this is what it would have shown: A four-and-a-half-foot-tall boy stands mashing and then pounding the elevator call button. Beside him is a man, maybe a foot taller, dressed in a shirt and tie and holding a lidded cup in each hand. Is it raining outside? If not, perhaps he just stepped from the shower and threw on his clothes without drying himself. His eyes shift this way and that, giving the impression that he is searching for somebody. Could it be this silver-haired gentleman? He's just walked up, looking very dapper in his tweed jacket and matching cap. He talks to the boy and lays a hand on the back of his head, scolding him probably, which is good, as somebody needed to. The other man, the wet one, is just standing there, holding the cups and trying to wipe his forehead with his sleeve at the same time. A lid pops off and something — it looks like coffee — spills down the front of his shirt. He leaps about, prancing almost, and pulls the fabric away from his skin. The boy seems angry now and says something. The older gentleman offers a handkerchief, and the man sets down one of his cups and runs — literally runs, panting — off camera, returning thirty seconds later with another lidded cup, a replacement. By this time the elevator has arrived. The gentleman holds open the door, and he and the boy wait as the man picks the other cup off the floor and joins them. Then the door closes, and they are gone.

"So, who have we got here?" the gentleman asked. His voice was jovial and enthusiastic. "What do you call yourself, big fella?"

"Michael," the boy said.

"Well, that's a grown-up name, isn't it."

Michael guessed that it was, and the man caught my eye and winked, the way people do when they're establishing a partnership. *We'll just put on the small fry, what do you say?* "I bet a big guy like you must have a lot of girlfriends," he said. "Is that true?"

"No."

"You *don't?* Well, what's the problem?"

"I don't know. I just don't have one. That's all," Michael said.

I had always hated it when men asked the girlfriend question. Not only was it corny, but it set you in their imaginations in a way that seemed private to me. Answer yes and they'd picture your wee courtship: the candlelit dinner of hot dogs and potato chips, the rumpled Snoopy sheets. Answer no and you were blue-balled, the frustrated bachelor of the second grade. It was an idea of children as miniature adults, which was about as funny to me as a dog in sunglasses.

"Well, there must be *someone* you have your eye on."

The boy did not answer, but the man

persisted in trying to draw him out. "Is Mommy sleeping in this morning?"

Again, nothing.

The man gave up and turned to me. "Your wife," he said. "I take it she's still in bed?"

He thought I was Michael's father, and I did not correct him. "Yes," I said. "She's upstairs . . . passed out." I don't know why I said this, or then again, maybe I do. The man had constructed a little family portrait, and there was a pleasure in defacing it. Here was Michael, here was Michael's dad, and now, here was Mom, lying facedown on the bathroom floor.

The elevator stopped on three, and the man tipped his hat. "All right, then," he said. "You two enjoy the rest of the morning." Michael had pressed the button for the fifth floor no less than twenty times, and now he gave it an extra few jabs just for good measure. We were alone now, and something unpleasant entered my mind.

Sometimes when I'm in a tight situation, I'll feel a need to touch somebody's head. It happens a lot on airplanes. I'll look at the person seated in front of me, and within a moment the idea will have grown from a possibility to a compulsion. There is no option — I simply have to do it. The easiest method is to make like I'm getting up, to grab the forward seat for support and just sort of pat the person's hair with my fingers. "Oh, I'm sorry," I say.

"No problem."

Most often I'll continue getting out of my seat, then walk to the back of the plane or go to the bathroom and stand there for a few minutes, trying to fight off what I know is inevitable: I need to touch the person's head again. Experience has taught me that you can do this three times before the head's owner either yells at you or rings for the flight attendant. "Is something wrong?" she'll ask.

"I don't think so, no."

"What do you mean 'no,' " the passenger will say. "This freak keeps touching my head."

"Is that true, sir?"

It's not always a head. Sometimes I need to touch a particular purse or briefcase. When I was a child this sort of compulsive behavior was my life, but now I practice it only if I'm in a situation where I can't smoke: planes — as I mentioned — and elevators.

Just touch the boy's head, I thought. *The old man did it, so why can't you?*

To remind myself that this is inappropriate only makes the voice more insistent. The thing must be done *because* it is inappropriate. If it weren't, there'd be no point in bothering with it.

He won't even notice it. Touch him now, quick.

Were we traveling a long distance, I would have lost the battle, but fortunately we weren't going far. The elevator arrived on the fifth floor and I scrambled out the door, set the coffees on the carpet, and lit a cigarette. "You're going to have to give me a minute here," I said.

"But my room's just down the hall. And this is nonsmoking."

"I know, I know."

"It's not good for you," he said.

"That's true for a lot of people," I told him. "But it *really is* good for me. Take my word for it."

He leaned against a door and removed the DO NOT DISTURB sign, studying it for a moment before sticking it in his back pocket.

I only needed to smoke for a minute, but realized when I was finished that there was no ashtray. Beside the elevator was a window, but of course it was sealed shut. Hotels. They do everything in their power to make you want to jump to your death, and then they make certain that you can't do it. "Are you finished with your cocoa?" I asked.

"No."

"Well, are you finished with the lid?"

"I guess so."

He handed it to me and I spit into the center — no easy task, as my mouth was completely dry. Fifty percent of my body water was seeping out my ass, and the other half was in transit.

"That's gross," he said.

"Yeah, well, you're just going to have to forgive me." I stubbed the cigarette into the spit, set the lid on the carpet, and picked up the coffees. "Okay. Where to?"

He pointed down a long corridor and I followed him, gnawing on a question that's been troubling me for years. What if you had a baby and you just . . . you just needed to touch it where you knew you shouldn't. I don't mean that you'd want to. You wouldn't *desire* the baby any more than you desire a person whose head you've just touched. The act would be compulsive rather than sexual, and while to you there'd be a big difference, you couldn't expect a prosecutor, much less an infant, to recognize it. You'd be a bad parent, and once the child could talk and you told it not to tell anyone, you would become a manipulator — a monster, basically — and the reason behind your actions would no longer matter.

The closer we got to the end of the hall, the more anxious I became. I had not laid a finger on the boy's head. I have never poked or prodded either a baby or a child, so why did I feel so dirty? Part of it was just my makeup, the deep-seated belief that I deserve a basement room, but a larger, uglier part had to do with the voices I hear on talk radio, and my tendency, in spite of myself, to pay them heed. The man in the elevator had not thought twice about asking Michael personal questions or about laying a hand on the back of his head. Because he was neither a priest nor a homosexual, he hadn't felt the need to watch himself, worrying that every word or gesture might be misinterpreted. He could unthinkingly wander the halls with a strange boy, while for me it amounted to a political act — an insistence that I was as good as the next guy. Yes, I am a homosexual; yes, I am soaking wet; yes, I sometimes feel an urge to touch people's heads, but still I can safely see a ten-year-old back to his room. It bothered me that I needed to prove something this elementary. And prove it to people whom I could never hope to convince.

"This is it," Michael said. From the other side of the door I heard the sound of a television. It was one of those Sunday-morning magazine programs, a weekly hour where all news is good news. Blind Jimmy Henderson coaches a volleyball team. An ailing groundhog is fitted for a back brace. That type of thing. The boy inserted his card key into the slot, and the door opened onto a bright, well-furnished room. It was twice the size of mine, with higher ceilings and a sitting area. One window framed a view of the lake, and the other a stand of scarlet maples.

"Oh, you're back," a woman said. She was clearly the boy's mother, as their profiles were identical, the foreheads easing almost imperceptively into blunt freckled noses. Both too had spiky blond hair, though for her I imagined the style was accidental, the result of the pillows piled behind her head. She was lying beneath the covers of a canopy bed, examining one of the many brochures scattered across the comforter. A man slept beside her, and when she spoke, he shifted slightly and covered his face with the crook of his arm.

"What took you so long?" She looked toward the open door, and her eyes widened as they met mine. "What the . . ."

There was a yellow robe at the foot of the bed, and the woman turned her back to me as she got up and stepped into it. Her son reached for the coffees, and I tightened my grip, unwilling to surrender what I'd come to think of as my props. They turned me from a stranger to a kindly stranger, and I'd seen myself holding them as his parents rounded on me, demanding to know what was going on.

"Give them to me," he said, and rather than making a scene, I relaxed my grip. The coffees were taken, and I felt my resolve starting to crumble. Empty-handed, I was just a creep, the spooky wet guy who'd crawled up from the basement. The woman crossed to the dresser, and as the door started to close she called out to me. "Hey," she said. "Wait a minute." I turned, ready to begin the fight of my life, and she stepped forward and pressed a dollar into my hand. "You people run a very nice hotel," she told me. "I just wish we could stay longer."

The door closed and I stood alone in the empty corridor, examining my tip and thinking, *Is that all?*

Who's the Chef?

"My boss has a rubber hand," I told our Parisian dinner guests following my one and only day of work. The French word for *boss* is our word for *chef,* so it sounded even better than I'd expected. A chef with a rubber hand. You'd think it would melt.

The guests leaned closer to the table, not sure if I was using the right word. "Your *chef?* Since when did you start working?" They turned to Hugh for confirmation. "He has a job?"

Thinking, I guess, that I wouldn't notice, Hugh set down his fork and mouthed the words "It's volunteer work." What irritated me was the manner in which he said it — not outright, but barely whispered, the way you might if your three-year-old was going on about his big day at school. "It's day care."

"Volunteer or not, I still had a chef," I said. "And his hand was made of rubber." I'd sat on this information for hours, had even rehearsed its delivery, double-checking all the important words in the dictionary. I don't know what I'd expected — but it definitely wasn't this.

"I'm sure it wasn't *actual* rubber," Hugh said. "It was probably some kind of plastic."

The friends agreed, but they hadn't seen my chef, hadn't watched as he thoughtlessly wedged a pencil between his manmade fingers. A plastic hand wouldn't have given quite so easily. A plastic hand would have made a different sound against the tabletop. "I know what I saw," I said. "It was rubber and it smelled like a pencil eraser."

If someone told me that his boss's hand smelled like a pencil eraser, I'd shut up and go with it, but Hugh was in one of his moods. "What, this guy let you smell his hand?"

"Well, no," I said. "Not exactly."

"Okay, then, it was plastic."

"So, what," I said, "is everything *not* held directly to your nose made out of plastic? Is that the rule now?" One of our joint New Year's resolutions was to stop bickering in front of company, but he was making it really hard. "The hand was rubber," I said. "Heavy rubber, like a tire."

"So it was inflatable?" The guests laughed at Hugh's little joke, and I took a moment to think the worse of them. An inflatable hand is preposterous and not worth imagining. Couldn't they see that?

"Look," I said, "this wasn't something I saw in a shop. I was right there, in the room with it."

"Fine," Hugh said. "So what else?"

"What do you mean, 'what else'?"

"Your volunteer job. So the boss had an artificial hand — what else?"

Let me explain that it isn't easy finding volunteer work in Paris. The government pays people to do just about everything, especially during an election year, and when I visited the benevolence center, the only thing available was a one-day job helping to guide the blind through one of the city's Metro stations. The program was run by my chef, who'd set up a temporary office in a small windowless room beside the ticket booth. It wasn't my fault that no blind people showed up. "Listen," I said, "I just spent six hours in a storage closet being ignored by a man with a rubber hand. What do you mean, 'What else?' What more do I need?"

The friends stared blankly, and I realized I'd been speaking in English.

"In French," Hugh said. "Say it in French."

It was one of those times when you really notice the difference between speaking and expressing yourself. I knew the words — *blind people, election year, storage closet* — but even when coupled with verbs and pronouns they didn't add up the way I needed them to. In English my sentences could perform double duty, saying both that I'd reported for volunteer work *and* that Hugh would be punished for not listening to the single most interesting thing that had happened to me since moving to Paris.

"Just forget it," I said.

"Suit yourself."

I left the table for a glass of water, and when I returned, Hugh was discussing Monsieur DiBiasio, the plumber hired to replace our bathroom sink.

"He's got one arm," I told the guests.

"No, he doesn't," Hugh said. "He's got two."

"Yes, but one of them doesn't work."

"Well, he's still *got* it," Hugh said. "It's *there*. It fills a sleeve."

He's always doing this, contradicting me in front of company. And so I did what I always do, which is ask a question and then deny him a chance to answer.

"Define *an arm*," I said. "If you're talking about the long, hairy thing that hangs from your shoulder, okay, he's got two, but if you're talking about a long hairy thing that moves around and actually *does* shit then he's got one, all right? I should know. I'm the one who carried the sink up three goddam flights of stairs. Me, not you."

The guests were getting uncomfortable, but I didn't care. Technically, Hugh was right, the plumber had two arms, but we weren't in a courtroom and there was no punishment for a little exaggeration. People like mental pictures; they give them something to do besides just listening. Hadn't we been through this? Instead of backing me up, he'd made me out to be a liar, and, oh, I hated him for that.

Once he'd destroyed my credibility with the one-armed plumber, it was pretty much over as far as the rubber hand was concerned. The guests weren't even thinking plastic anymore, they were thinking actual working hand, made of flesh and bone and muscle. The mental picture had been erased and they'd never understand that a hand is defined by its movement rather than its shape. The chef's had fingernails, creases — you probably could have read the palm — but it was pink and stiffish, like a false hand you might use when teaching a dangerous animal to shake. I don't know how it attached or where, but I'm fairly certain he could take it off without too much trouble. While sitting there, just the two of us, waiting for blind people who never showed, I imagined how the hand might look positioned on a bed-side table, if that was where he kept it. There was probably no point in wearing it to bed, the thing wasn't particularly helpful; the fingers didn't open and close. It was just a deception, like a hairpiece or a false eyelash.

The dinner conversation staggered on, but the evening was already shot. Anyone could see that. In another few minutes the guests would look at their watches and say something about their babysitter. Coats would be retrieved and we'd stand in the hallway saying good-bye again and again as the guests made their way down the stairs. I would clear the table and Hugh would do the dishes, neither of us speaking and both of us wondering if this just might be the one to do it. "I hear you guys broke up over a plastic hand," people would say, and my rage would renew itself. The argument would continue until one of us died, and even then it would manage to wage on. If I went first, my tombstone would read IT

WAS RUBBER. He'd likely take the adjacent plot and buy a larger tombstone reading NO, IT WAS PLASTIC.

Dead or alive, I'd have no peace, and so I let it go, the way you have to when you're totally dependent on somebody. In the coming weeks I'd picture the hand waving good-bye or shooting into the air to hail a taxi — going about its little business as I went about mine. Hugh would ask why I was smiling and I'd say, "Oh, no reason," and leave it at that.

Baby Einstein

My mother and I were on the beach, rubbing oil into each other's backs and guessing who in the family would be the first to have children. "I think it will be Lisa," I said. This was in the early 1970s. Lisa was maybe fourteen years old and while she wasn't necessarily maternal, she did do things according to their order. Getting married was what came after graduating from college, and having a baby was what came after getting married. "Mark my words," I said, "by the age of twenty-six Lisa will have" — a trio of ghost crabs approached an abandoned sandwich, and I took them as a sign — "Lisa will have three children."

It felt very prophetic, but my mother dismissed it. "No," she said. "Gretchen will be the first." She squinted toward her second daughter, who stood on the shore, pitching meat scraps to a flock of gulls. "It's written on her hips. It will be Gretchen, then Lisa, then Tiffany."

"What about Amy?" I asked.

My mother thought for a moment. "Amy won't have a child," she said. "Amy will have a monkey."

I did not include myself in the baby prophecy, as I couldn't imagine a time when homosexuals, either through adoption or the procurement of a rented womb, could create families of their own. I did not include my brother, because every time I saw him he was destroying something, not by accident but willfully, gleefully. He'd dismember his baby, with every intention of putting it back together, but then something would come up — a karate movie, the chance to eat two dozen tacos — and the reconstruction would be forgotten about.

Neither my mother nor I could have imagined that the boy smashing bottles on the path to our cottage would be the first and only one in the family to have a child. By the time it happened, she would be long gone and my sisters, my father, and I would have to bear the shock alone. "It happened so fast!" we would say to one another, speaking as if Paul was like us and preceded every action with ten years of discussion. But he's not like us, and to hear him tell it, the debate ended with a simple "Take them panties off." Kathy did, and shortly after getting married, he called me to announce that she was pregnant.

"Since when?" I asked.

Paul held the phone away from his mouth and yelled into the other room. "Mama, what time is it?"

"You're calling her 'Mama'?"

He yelled for her again, and I told him that if it was four o'clock in Paris, it was ten a.m. in Raleigh. "So how long has she been pregnant?"

He figured it had been about nine hours. They had used one of those home-testing kits. The previous evening the result had been negative. This morning it was positive, and Kathy had become Mama, which would eventually change to Big Mama, and later, for no particular reason, Mama D.

When my friend Andy and his wife discovered they were going to have a baby, they kept it a secret for eight weeks. This, I learned, is fairly common. The fetus was minute — a congregation of loitering cells — and as with anything that informal, there was a good chance that it might disperse. A miscarriage turned would-be parents into objects of pity, and you didn't want to set yourselves up too early.

"I don't mean to discourage you," I said

to Paul, "but maybe you two should keep this to yourselves for a while."

He coughed, and I understood that he and Kathy had been on the phone for hours, that I was probably the last to be called.

What I considered a reasonable degree of caution he dismissed as "nay-sayery."

"I'll chain its ass down if I have to, but ain't no baby of mine going to forsake the womb."

After hanging up, he went to the store and bought a nursing chair, a changing table, and a bib reading I LOVE MY DADDY. I thought of those children you sometimes see at demonstrations. ANOTHER TODDLER FOR PEACE, their T-shirts read, or, my favorite, I'M SO GLAD MY MOMMY DIDN'T ABORT ME.

"Shouldn't you wait until the baby can talk and say that kind of thing for itself?" I asked. "Or maybe at least hold out until it has a real neck. What are you doing buying bibs?"

The next time he called he was at the counter of a toy store charging a set of *Baby Einstein* videos. "I don't care if it's a boy or a girl, but this little son of a bitch is going to have brains."

"Well, it's sure not going to get them

from his parents," I said. "Kathy hasn't even gone to the doctor and already you've got videos?"

"A crib, too, and I'll tell you what, this shit's expensive as hell."

"Well, so is calling France on a cell phone at eleven o'clock on a Wednesday morning," I said, though again, I don't know who I thought I was talking to. My brother can't survive unless he's breathing into a telephone. If you're an enemy, he'll call only once a day, but if you're a family member and on relatively good speaking terms, you're guaranteed to hear from him once every eight hours or so. There's the money he spends calling us, and then there's the money my sisters and I spend calling one another to talk about how much our brother calls us.

When the pregnancy became official, he called even more. "Big day, Hoss. We're taking Mama in to get her Corky test." Corky was a character from an early-nineties TV program and was played by a young man with Down syndrome. My sister Lisa got the message as well and wasn't sure if the fetus was being tested for a triploid twenty-first chromosome or the possibility that it might grow up to become an actor. "I'm pretty sure they can determine the drama gene now," she said.

By the sixth month the only surprise left was the baby's sex. Paul and his wife speculated, but neither of them wanted to know for certain. It was, they said, bad luck, but how was it any unluckier than furnishing a nursery or preaddressing the birth-announcement cards? Like everyone else in the family, I kept a list of possible names and called every so often to offer them up: Dusty, Ginger, Kaneesha — all of them rejected. The contractors and carpenters my brother works with suggested names as well, most of them inspired by the pending war or the image of America as a tarnished but still shining beacon. Liberty was popular, as was Glory, the slightly Italian-sounding Vendetta, and Kick Saddam's Ass, which, as my father pointed out, didn't leave much room for a middle name. All of his suggestions were Greek and were offered with a complete disregard of the inevitable taunting they would inspire. "You can't enter the third grade with a name like Hercules," Lisa told him. "The same is true of Lesbos, I don't care how pretty it sounds."

Then there was the pressure of naming the child after one of its grandparents. Lou and Sharon were options, but there was also Kathy's family to consider. "Oh, right," my sister Amy said. "Them." The Wilsons were nice people, but we saw them as interlopers, potential threats standing between us and what we'd come to think of as the Sedaris baby. "Don't Kathy's parents already *have* a grandchild?" I asked, speaking as if a grandchild were like a Social Security number or a spinal column — something you needed only one of. We decided they were greedy and capable of anything, yet when the time came to compete, we completely dropped the ball. Their team was out in full force when the baby was born, while we were represented by only Lisa and our father. Kathy was in labor for fifteen hours before the doctors decided to perform a cesarean. The news was delivered to the waiting room, and when the time came my father looked at his watch, saying, "Well, I guess they should be carving her up right about now." Then he went home to feed his dog. By this point, naming the child Lou was on par with naming it Adolph or Beelzebub, but all three were disqualified when the baby turned out to be a girl.

They named her Madelyn, which was shortened to Maddy by the time she reached the incubator. I was in a hotel in

Portland, Oregon, at the time and received the news from my brother, who called from the recovery room. His voice was soft and melodic, not much more than a whisper. "Mama's got some tubes sticking out of her pussy, but it ain't no big thing," he said. "She's lying back, little Maddy's sucking on her titty just as happy as she can be." This was the new, gentler Paul: same vocabulary, but the tone was sweeter and seasoned with a sense of wonder. The cesarean had been unpleasant, but after bemoaning the months wasted in Lamaze class, he grew reflective. "Some is cut loose and others come out on their own self, but take heed, brother: having a baby is a fucking miracle."

"Did you just say, 'Take heed'?" I asked.

Kathy returned home later that week, but there were problems. Her legs were swollen. She couldn't breathe. An ambulance carried her to the emergency room, where they drained thirty pounds of fluid from her body: accumulated water and, to her great disappointment, her breast milk. "It'll still continue to come in," Paul said, "but because of all the medication she's on, we're going to have to pump and dump." This was a medical term he'd picked up from the doctor, who announced in the same breath that Kathy could not have any more children. "Her heart's too weak, but can you believe that shit?" His new voice temporarily disappeared. "Breaking bad on Mama D when she's on tap and already scared half to death? I said, 'Fucker, begone with your pump-dumping, Pakistan-community-college-attending ass. I'm getting me a specialist.' "

"It's interesting," I told him, "that in the nineteenth century they used puppies to drain a woman's breast milk."

Paul said nothing.

"I just thought it was a pleasant image," I said.

He agreed, but his mind was on other things: his sick wife, the baby he was caring for on his own, and the second, hoped-for child he knew now they could never have. "Puppies," he said. "I bet they could really drain your ass."

I flew to Raleigh two weeks after the baby was born, and my father, unshaven and looking all of his eighty years, arrived half an hour late to pick me up at the airport. "You'll have to excuse me if I'm a little out of it," he said. "I'm not feeling too hot, and it took me a while to find my medicine." It seemed he had a little infection and was fighting it by taking antibiotics originally prescribed for his Great Dane. "Pills are pills," he said. "Whether they're for a dog or a human, they're the same damned thing."

I thought it was funny and later told my sister Lisa, who did not get quite the kick out of it that I did. "I think that's horrible," she said. "I mean, how is Sophie supposed to get any better when Dad's taking all her medicine?"

Along with a stained T-shirt my father wore a pair of torn jeans and a baseball cap marked with the emblem of a heavy-metal band. I asked about it, and he shrugged, saying he'd found the hat in a parking lot.

"Do you think *Kathy's* father dresses like a roadie for Iron Maiden?" I asked.

"I don't give a damn what he wears," my father said.

"Do you think that when *he* gets sick, he just runs down to Petco and self-medicates?"

"Probably not, but what the hell difference does it make?"

"Just asking."

"And what," my father said, "you think you're going to win Best Uncle award by holing up in France, flipping pancakes with your little boyfriend?"

"Pancakes?"

"Well, whatever they call them," he said. "Crepes." He lurched from the curb, using his free hand to adjust the oversize glasses he'd bought in the seventies and had recently rediscovered in a drawer. On the way to Paul's house I told him a story I'd heard in one of the airports. A new mother had approached the security checkpoint carrying two servings of prepumped breast milk, and the goon in charge made her open both bottles and drink from them.

"Get out of here," my father said.

"No," I told him. "It's true. They want to make sure that whatever you're carrying isn't poison or some kind of an explosive. That's why sperm donors have taken to traveling Greyhound."

"It's a lousy world," he said.

Suggestions of how to improve this lousy world were displayed upon his rear bumper. My father and I do not agree politically, so when riding with him I tend to slump down in the seat, ashamed to be seen in what my sisters and I call *the Bushmobile*. It's like being a child all over again. Dad at the wheel and my head so low, I'm unable to see out the window. "Are we there yet?" I ask. "Are we there?"

Madelyn was asleep when we arrived, and Paul, my father, and I gathered around the crib to adore her in soft voices. One of them suggested that she resembled my mother, but to me she just looked like a baby, not the cute kind you see on diaper commercials but the raw, wrinkled kind that resemble bitter old men.

"It'll be different when her hair comes in," Paul said. "Some babies is born with it, but it's less gnarlier for the mother when they're bawl-headed." He waved his hands before his daughter's closed eyes. "It's the mothers I think about. Can you imagine what that must be like, having something inside you that's all fur-bearing and shit?"

"Well, fur and hair are different things," my father said. "Having a raccoon inside you, all right, I see your point, but a few hairs never hurt anybody."

Paul shuddered and I told him about a recent documentary, the story of a boy who'd been surgically separated from his secret interior twin. It lived inside of him for seven years, a little dummy with no heart or brain of its own. "That's fine, or whatever," I whispered, "but it had this really long hair."

"Like, how long?" Paul asked.

In truth I hadn't seen the documentary, just read about it. "Really long," I said. "About three feet."

"That's like having a fucking Willie Nelson doll living inside you," Paul said.

"It's a bunch of baloney," my father said.

"No, really. I saw it."

"Like hell you did."

The baby raised a fist to her mouth, and Paul lowered his head into the crib. "That's just your uncle Faggot and your raggedy-assed granddaddy talking some of their old stupid bullshit," he said. And it sounded so . . . comforting.

When my father left, Paul heated up a serving of formula. The baby woke up, and Kathy settled her onto the sofa, where the four of us watched videos taken in the hospital. That my brother had not filmed the actual cesarean led me to believe that someone had expressly forbidden it, perhaps for legal or sanitary reasons. There was a blank spot between the arrival of the doctor and the purple-faced baby wailing like an urgent call at the end of her umbilical cord. As if to make up for the missing seven minutes, the recovery-room footage goes on forever. Kathy drinks from a plastic cup of water. A nurse wanders in to change the bandages. Often my sister-in-law is naked or topless, but if she was bothered by the sight of herself playing on a wide-screen TV, she did not show it. Sometimes she held the camera, and we saw Paul in his cutoff shorts and promotional T-shirt, a baseball cap turned backward on his head.

The two of them had watched this video dozens of times, but still they sat enraptured. "Here's where that nurse's aide comes in," Kathy said. Paul turned off the volume and as the woman stuck her head through the door he lip-synched her voice.

"Look like evabody in here asleep."

"Do it again," Kathy said.

"Look like evabody in here asleep."

"Again."

"Look like evabody in here asleep."

Further along there was footage of the baby's first bowel movement. It looked like tar, and when the last of it had seeped out, Paul hit the reverse button and watched as the puddle contracted and crept back into his daughter's body. "You see how dark that shit is?" he said. "I mean to tell you this little baby's *advanced*."

He held Madelyn up to the TV screen and she gave a little, two-syllable cry that sounded to Paul like "whoopee!" but I interpreted as something closer to "help meeeee."

People who have nothing to prove offer practical baby gifts: sturdy cotton rompers made to withstand the cycle of vomit and regular washing. People who are competing for the titles of best-loved aunts and uncles — people like my sisters and me — send satin pants and delicate hand-crafted sweaters accompanied by notes reading "P.S. The fur collar is detachable." The baby is photographed in each new outfit, and I receive pictures almost daily. In them my brother and his wife look not like parents but like backwoods kidnappers, secretly guarding the heiress to a substantial cashmere fortune.

Between the still cameras and the video cameras, Madelyn's every move is documented and presented as "Baby's First . . ." Baby's First Beach Trip doubled as Baby's First Hurricane. Supported by her mother, she looks past the bent sea oats and out toward the blackening sky, her face creased in an expression of wisdom and concern never seen on either of her parents. The Fourth of July, Halloween, Thanksgiving: these are just days to her, but Paul and Kathy, their logic paralyzed by love, insist that their daughter is cognizant and as excited as they are.

On Baby's First Day of Winter Madelyn sat before a video of *A Christmas Carol*, then watched as, in imitation of a Victorian gentleman, my brother applied a pair of muttonchop sideburns. This was accomplished not with a disguise kit, but simply, using two strips of raw bacon that ran along his jawline and remained in place for minutes at a time through the miracle of fat against human flesh. Then Paul got out the ladder and taped Christmas lights to the front of his house. They too were short-term, collapsing into the bushes moments after the picture was taken. The baby, of course, already knew what she would be getting. Gifts were presented the moment my brother returned from the store. Baby's First Pop-Up Book. Baby's First Talking Doll. One of her presents was a phonetics aid called the Alphabet Pal. Press *D*, for example, and the machine recites the letter. Press *D*, then *A*, then *D* again, and it connects the letters into a clumsily pronounced word. "Duh-Aah-Duh." It sounds like someone with a mechanical voice box and is far too advanced for a child Madelyn's age. She wanted nothing to do with it, so by Christmas morning it had become my brother's toy. He is determined to make it curse, but the Alphabet Pal is crafty and decent and soon figured out what he was up to. *M-o-t-h-e-r* is fine, but try following it with *f-u-c-k-e-r* and by the second letter the machine will giggle and, in a natural, little-girl voice, give you a piece of its mind. "Ha ha ha *ha*. You're silly!" "I can't even get it to say *dick*," he says, "and that's a goddam *name*."

My sister-in-law's condition calls for her to sleep through the night, so when Madelyn wakes at two and three and five a.m., it is Paul's job to feed her or change her, or carry her around the house, begging her to lighten up. There's no point in going to bed, so he kicks his pillow from room to room and collapses on the floor in front of her crib or the swinging chair that sits in the dining room. When the last of my sisters has hit the sack, he dials me up and holds the receiver to his daughter's mouth. For months I listened to her cry long-distance, but then she got a little older and learned how to laugh and coo and sigh in that satisfied baby way that makes me understand how some could bring a child into this lousy world of ours.

"She'll turn on him sooner or later," my

father says. "Just you wait. In a couple of years Madelyn won't want anything to do with him."

I look into the future and see my brother's face, impossibly middle-aged. His daughter has rejected all of his values, and stands now on the dais of a major university, the valedictorian preparing to deliver her commencement speech. What will she think when her dad stands in the aisle, releasing a hog call and raising his T-shirt to reveal the jiggling message painted upon his bare stomach? Will she turn away, as my father predicts, or might she remember all the nights she awoke to discover him: this slob, this lump, this silly drooling toy asleep at her feet.

Nuit of the Living Dead

I was on the front porch, drowning a mouse in a bucket when this van pulled up, which was strange. On an average day a total of fifteen cars might pass the house, but no one ever stops, not unless they live here. And this was late, three o'clock in the morning. The couple across the street are asleep by nine, and from what I can tell, the people next door turn in an hour or so later. There are no streetlamps in our village in Normandy, so when it's dark, it's really dark. And when it's quiet, you can hear everything.

"Did I tell you about the burglar who got stuck in the chimney?" That was the big story last summer. One time it happened in the village at the bottom of the hill, the pretty one bisected by a river, and another time it took place fifteen miles in the opposite direction. I heard the story from four people, and each time it happened in a different place.

"So this burglar," people said. "He tried the doors and windows and when those wouldn't open, he climbed up onto the roof."

It was always a summer house, a cottage owned by English people whose names no one seemed to remember. The couple left in early September and returned ten months later to find a shoe in their fireplace. "Is this yours?" the wife asked her husband.

The two of them had just arrived. There were beds to be made and closets to air out, so between one thing and another the shoe was forgotten. It was early June, chilly, and as night fell, the husband decided to light a fire.

At this point in the story the tellers were beside themselves, their eyes aglow, as if reflecting the light of a campfire. "Do you honestly expect me to believe this?" I'd say. "I mean, *really.*"

At the beginning of the summer the local paper devoted three columns to a Camembert-eating contest. Competitors were pictured, hands behind their backs, their faces buried in soft, sticky cheese. This on the front page. In an area so hard up for news, I think a death by starvation might command the headlines for, oh, about six years.

"But wait," I'm told. "There's more!"

As the room filled with smoke, the husband stuck a broom up the chimney. Something was blocking the flue, and he poked at it again and again, dislodging the now skeletal burglar, who fell feetfirst into the flames.

There was always a pause here, a break between the story and the practical questions that would ultimately destroy it. "So who was this burglar?" I'd ask. "Did they identify his body?"

He was a Gypsy, a drifter, and, on two occasions, an Arab. No one remembered exactly where he was from. "But it's true," they said. "You can ask anyone," by which they meant the neighbor who had told them, or the person they themselves had told five minutes earlier.

I never believed that a burglar starved to death in a chimney. I don't believe that his skeleton dropped onto the hearth. But I do believe in spooks, especially when Hugh is away and I'm left alone in the country. During the war our house was occupied by Nazis. The former owner died in the bedroom, as did the owner before her, but it's not their ghosts that I worry about. It's silly, I know, but what frightens me is the possibility of zombies, former townspeople wandering about in pus-covered night-gowns. There's a church graveyard a quarter of a mile away, and were its residents to lurch out the gate and take a left, ours would be the third house they would stumble upon. Lying in bed with all the lights on, I draw up contingency plans on the off chance they might come a-callin'. The attic seems a wise hideout, but I'd have to secure the door, which would take time, time you do not have when zombies are steadily working their way through your windows.

I used to lie awake for hours, but now, if Hugh's gone for the night, I'll just stay up and keep myself busy: writing letters, cleaning the oven, replacing missing buttons. I won't put in a load of laundry, because the machine is too loud and would drown out other, more significant noises — namely, the shuffling footsteps of the living dead.

On this particular night, the night the van pulled up, I was in what serves as the combination kitchen/living room, trying to piece together a complex model of the Visible Man. The body was clear plastic, a shell for the organs, which ranged in color from bright red to a dull, liverish purple.

We'd bought it as a birthday gift for a thirteen-year-old boy, the son of a friend, who pronounced it *null*, meaning "worthless, unacceptable." The summer before, he'd wanted to be a doctor, but over the next few months he seemed to have changed his mind, deciding instead that he might like to design shoes. I suggested that he at least keep the feet, but when he turned up his nose we gave him twenty euros and decided to keep the model for ourselves. I had just separated the digestive system when I heard a familiar noise coming from overhead, and dropped half the colon onto the floor.

There's a walnut tree in the side yard, and every year Hugh collects the fruit and lays it on the attic floor to dry. Shortly thereafter, the mice come in. I don't know how they climb the stairs, but they do, and the first thing on their list is to take Hugh's walnuts. They're much too big to be carried by mouth, so instead they roll them across the floor, pushing them toward the nests they build in the tight spaces between the walls and the eaves. Once there, they discover that the walnuts won't fit, and while I find this to be comic, Hugh thinks differently and sets the attic with traps I normally spring before the mice can get to them. Were they rats, it would be different, but a couple of mice? "Come on," I say. "What could be cuter?"

Sometimes, when the rolling gets on my nerves, I'll turn on the attic light and make like I'm coming up the stairs. This quiets them for a while, but on this night the trick didn't work. The noise kept up but sounded like something being dragged rather than rolled. A shingle? A heavy piece of toast? Again I turned on the attic light, and when the noise continued I went upstairs and found a mouse caught in one of the traps Hugh had set. The steel bar had come down on his back, and he was pushing himself in a tight circle, not in a death throe, but with a spirit of determination, an effort to work within this new set of boundaries. "I can live with this," he seemed to be saying. "Really. Just give me a chance."

I couldn't leave him that way, so I scooted the trapped mouse into a cardboard box and carried him down onto the front porch. The fresh air, I figured, would do him some good, and once released, he could run down the stairs and into the yard, free from the house that now held such bitter memories. I should have lifted the bar with my fingers, but instead, worried that he might try to bite me, I held the trap down with my foot and attempted to pry it open with the end of a metal ruler. Which was stupid. No sooner had the bar been raised than it snapped back, this time on the mouse's neck. My next three attempts were equally punishing, and when finally freed, he staggered onto the doormat, every imaginable bone broken in at least four different places. Anyone could see that he was not going to get any better. Not even a vet could have fixed this mouse, and so, to put him out of his misery, I decided to drown him.

The first step, and for me the most difficult, was going into the cellar to get the bucket. This involved leaving the well-lit porch, walking around to the side of the house, and entering what is surely the bleakest and most terrifying hole in all of Europe. Low ceiling, stone walls, a dirt floor stamped with paw prints. I never go in without announcing myself. "Hyaa!" I yell. "Hyaa. Hyaa!" It's the sound my father makes when entering his toolshed, the cry of cowboys as they round up dogies, and it suggests a certain degree of authority. Snakes, bats, weasels — it's time to head up and move on out. When retrieving the bucket, I carried a flashlight in each hand, holding them low, like pistols. Then I kicked in the door — "Hyaa! Hyaa!" — grabbed what I was looking for, and ran. I was back on the porch in less than a minute, but it took much longer for my hands to stop shaking.

The problem with drowning an animal — even a crippled one — is that it does not want to cooperate. This mouse had nothing going for him, and yet he struggled, using what, I don't really know. I tried to hold him down with a broom handle but it wasn't the right tool for the job and he kept breaking free and heading back to the surface. A creature that determined, you want to let it have its way, but this was for the best, whether he realized it or not. I'd just managed to pin his tail to the bottom of the bucket when this van drove up and stopped in front of the house. I say "van," but it was more like a miniature bus, with windows and three rows of seats. The headlights were on high, and the road before them appeared black and perfect.

After a moment or two the driver's window rolled down, and a man stuck his head into the pool of light spilling from the porch. "Bonsoir," he called. He said it the way a man in a lifeboat might yell, "Ahoy!" to a passing ship, giving the impression that he was very happy to see me. As he opened the door, a light came on and I could see five people seated behind him, two men and three women, each looking at me with the same expression of relief. All were adults, perhaps in their sixties or early seventies, and all of them had white hair.

The driver referred to a small book he held in his hand. Then he looked back at me and attempted to recite what he had just read. It was French, but just barely, pronounced phonetically, with no understanding of where the accents lay.

"Do you speak English?" I asked.

The man clapped his hands and turned around in his seat. "He speaks English!" The news was greeted with a great deal of excitement and then translated for one of the women, who apparently did not understand the significance. Meanwhile, my mouse had popped back to the surface and was using his good hand to claw at the sides of the bucket.

"We are looking for a particular place," the driver said. "A house we are renting with friends." He spoke loudly and with a slight accent. Dutch, I thought, or maybe Scandinavian.

I asked what town the house was in, and he said that it was not in a town, just a willage.

"A what?"

"A willage," he repeated.

Either he had a speech impediment or the letter *v* did not exist in his native language. Whatever the case, I wanted him to say it again.

"I'm sorry," I said. "But I couldn't quite hear you."

"A *willage*," he said. "Some friends have rented a house in a little willage and we can't seem to find it. We were supposed to be there hours ago, but now we are quite lost. Do you know the area?"

I said that I did, but drew a blank when he called out the name. There are countless small villages in our part of Normandy, clusters of stone buildings hidden by forests or knotted at the end of unpaved roads. Hugh might have known the place the man was looking for, but because I don't drive, I tend not to pay too much attention. "I have a map," the man said. "Do you think you could perhaps look at it?"

He stepped from the van and I saw that he was wearing a white nylon tracksuit, the pants puffy and gathered tight at the ankles. You'd expect to find sneakers attached to such an outfit, but instead he wore a pair of black loafers. The front gate was open, and as he made his way up the stairs, I remembered what it was that I'd been doing, and I thought of how strange it might look. It occurred to me to meet the man halfway, but by this time he had already reached the landing and was offering his hand in a gesture of friendship. We shook, and on hearing the faint, lapping noise, he squinted down into the bucket. "Oh," he said. "I see that you have a little swimming mouse." His tone did not invite explanation, and so I offered none. "My wife and I have a dog," he continued. "But we did not bring it with us. Too much trouble."

I nodded and he held out his map, a Xerox of a Xerox marked with arrows and annotated in a language I did not recognize. "I think I've got something better in the house," I said, and at my invitation, he followed me inside.

An unexpected and unknown visitor allows you to see a familiar place as if for the very first time. I'm thinking of the meter reader rooting through the kitchen at eight a.m., the Jehovah's Witness suddenly standing in your living room. "Here," they seem to say. "Use *my* eyes. The focus is much keener." I had always thought of our main room as cheerful, but walking through the door, I saw that I was mistaken. It wasn't dirty or messy, but like being awake when all decent people are fast asleep, there was something slightly suspicious about it. I looked at the Visible Man spread out on the table. The pieces lay in the shadow of a large taxidermied chicken that seemed to be regarding them, determining which organ might be the most appetizing. The table itself was pleasant to look at — oak and hand-hewn — but the chairs surrounding it were mismatched and in various states of disrepair. On the back of one hung a towel marked with the emblem of the Los Angeles County Coroner's Office. It had been a gift, not bought personally, but still it was there, leading the eye to an adjacent daybed, upon which lay two copies of a sordid true-crime magazine I purportedly buy to help me with my French. The cover of the latest issue pictured a young Belgian woman, a camper beaten to death with a cinder block. IS THERE A SERIAL KILLER IN *YOUR* REGION? the headline asked. The second copy was opened to the crossword puzzle I'd attempted earlier in the evening.

One of the clues translated to "female sex organ," and in the space provided I had written the word for *vagina*. It was the first time I had ever answered a French crossword puzzle question, and in celebration I had marked the margins with bright exclamation points.

There seemed to be a theme developing, and everything I saw appeared to substantiate it: the almanac of guns and firearms suddenly prominent on the bookshelf, the meat cleaver lying for no apparent reason upon a photograph of our neighbor's grandchild.

"It's more of a summer home," I said, and the man nodded. He was looking now at the fireplace, which was slightly taller than he was. I tend to see only the solid stone hearth and high oak mantel, but he was examining the meat hooks hanging from the clotted black interior.

"Every other house we passed was dark," he said. "We've been driving I think for hours, just looking for someone who was awake. We saw your lights, the open door . . ." His words were familiar from innumerable horror movies, the wayward soul announcing himself to the count, the mad scientist, the werewolf, moments before he changes.

"I hate to bother you, really."

"Oh, it's no bother, I was just drowning a mouse. Come in, please."

"So," the man said, "you say you have a map?"

I had several, and pulled the most detailed from a drawer containing, among other things, a short length of rope and a novelty pen resembling a dismembered finger. *Where does all this stuff come from?* I asked myself. There's a low cabinet beside the table, and pushing aside the delicate skull of a baby monkey, I spread the map upon the surface, identifying the road outside our house and then the village the man was looking for. It wasn't more than ten miles away. The route was fairly simple, but still I offered him the map, knowing he would feel better if he could refer to it on the road.

"Oh no," he said, "I couldn't," but I insisted, and watched from the porch as he carried it down the stairs and into the idling van. "If you have any problems, you know where I live," I said. "You and your friends can spend the night here if you like. Really, I mean it. I have plenty of beds." The man in the tracksuit waved good-bye, and then he drove down the hill, disappearing behind the neighbor's pitched roof.

The mouse that had fought so hard against my broom handle had lost his second wind and was floating, lifeless now, on the surface of the water. I thought of emptying the bucket into the field behind the house, but without the van, its headlights, and the comforting sound of the engine, the area beyond the porch seemed too menacing. The inside of the house suddenly seemed just as bad, and so I stood there, looking out at what I'd now think of as my willage. When the sun came up I would bury my dead and fill the empty bucket with hydrangeas, a bit of life and color, so perfect for the table. So pleasing to the eye.

About the Author

David Sedaris is the author of *Me Talk Pretty One Day*, *Naked*, *Barrel Fever*, and *Holidays on Ice* and is a regular contributor to Public Radio International's "This American Life."

The employees of Thorndike Press hope you have enjoyed this Large Print book. All our Thorndike and Wheeler Large Print titles are designed for easy reading, and all our books are made to last. Other Thorndike Press Large Print books are available at your library, through selected bookstores, or directly from us.

For information about titles, please call:

(800) 223-1244

or visit our Web site at:

www.gale.com/thorndike
www.gale.com/wheeler

To share your comments, please write:

Publisher
Thorndike Press
295 Kennedy Memorial Drive
Waterville, ME   04901